CASE STUDIES IN
CULTURAL ANTHROPOLOGY

GENERAL EDITORS
George and Louise Spindler
STANFORD UNIVERSITY

A GUADALCANAL SOCIETY

The Kaoka Speakers

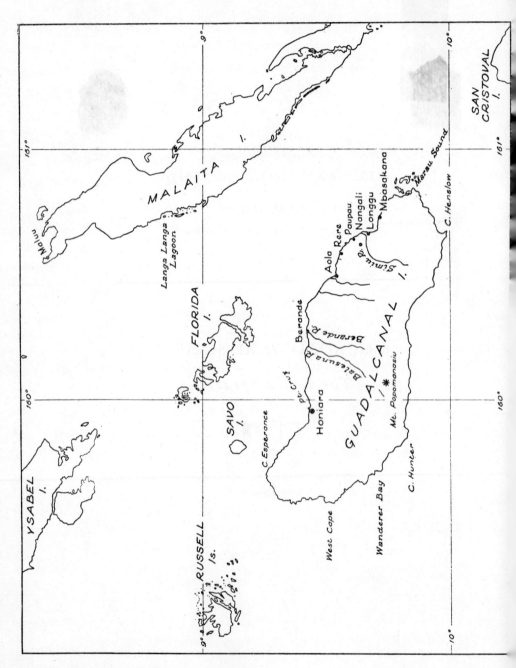

Guadalcanal and the surrounding Solomon Islands.

A GUADALCANAL SOCIETY
The Kaoka Speakers

By

IAN HOGBIN

University of Sydney

HOLT, RINEHART AND WINSTON

NEW YORK   CHICAGO   SAN FRANCISCO   TORONTO   LONDON

The field work on which this book is based was carried out while I held a Fellowship of the Australian National Research Council, to which body I wish to express my thanks.

I am grateful also for the help I received from F. N. Ashley (Resident Commissioner of the British Solomon Island Protectorate), from C. Wilson (District Officer of Guadalcanal), from F. R. Hewitt (Island Manager of Lever's Pacific Plantations), and from R. W. Swallow (Manager of Kaukau Estate).

I used the material in Chapter 7 as part of my Marett Memorial Lecture, "Morality without Religion," delivered at Exeter College, Oxford, in February 1961.

Ian Hogbin

Foreword

About the Series

These case studies in cultural anthropology are designed to bring to students and other interested readers insights into the richness and complexity of human life as it is lived in different ways and in different places. They are written by men and women who have lived in the societies they write about, and who are professionally trained as observers and interpreters of human behavior. The authors are also teachers, and in writing their books they have kept the students who will read them foremost in their minds. It is our belief that when an understanding of ways of life very different from one's own is gained, abstractions and generalizations about social structure, cultural values, subsistence techniques, and other universal categories of human social behavior become meaningful.

About the Author

Ian Hogbin is a Reader in Anthropology at the University of Sydney, Sydney, Australia.

He began his study of anthropology with Radcliffe-Brown, who founded the anthropology department at the University of Sydney, and his earliest field work was carried out under Radcliffe-Brown's supervision in Ontong-Java, a Polynesian colony in the Solomon Islands. Some of the results were published in his book *Law and Order in Polynesia.* He then went to London to work with Malinowski, at whose suggestion he returned to the Solomons, where he stayed in Guadalcanal and afterwards in Malaita. Subsequently, he made an investigation of the people of Wogeo, an island off the north coast of New Guinea.

During World War II he served in the Solomon Islands Defence Force and later in the Australian Army in New Guinea as an adviser on native rehabilitation problems. He continued working in New Guinea, and, in 1963, published the second of two volumes on the Busama villagers, who occupy a settlement near the town of Lae.

The Royal Anthropological Institute of Great Britain awarded him the Wellcome Medal for a work in applied anthropology in 1944 and the Rivers Medal for field work in 1945. He delivered the Munro Lectures at the University of Edinburgh in 1949, the Josiah Mason Lecturers at the University of Birmingham in 1953, and the Marett Memorial Lecture at Oxford in 1961. The University of

Melbourne awarded two of his books (*Transformation Scene* and *Social Change*) the Harbison-Higinbotham Prize.

About the Book

This is an unusually well-rounded presentation of a way of life, with all the major dimensions of cultural patterning and social structuring given substantial attention. The author gives the reader an exceptionally clear picture of the major social groups in this Guadalcanal society—the clan and subclan, village, hamlet, household, and family—the composition of these groupings, and their functions. He provides us with an excellent description of child rearing: how the values of generosity and respect for property are gently inculcated; the kinds of punishment, threats and rewards employed to bring about desired behavior; how the rules of kinship are learned; how technical skills are acquired. His chapter on religion gives us an understanding of the relationships between the spirits of the dead and the clans of the living, between beliefs and ritual behavior, and of the relationships between religion, magic, and technology. His treatment of conflict shows how it originates among the people of Guadalcanal, describes the involvements of groups in conflict situations, the settlement procedures, the role of sorcery, and the remedies for sorcery. This chapter leads us smoothly into his analysis of the headman's role, and how this status is achieved in Guadalcanal society. Throughout, the author consistently applies a sophisticated functional analysis to the interrelationships and interdependency among the various dimensions of belief, behavior, and social structuring that together constitute this way of life as a whole.

GEORGE AND LOUISE SPINDLER
General Editors

Stanford, California
1964

Contents

Preparing the food
for a feast.

Loading an overseas canoe for a
trading voyage.

A dance rehearsal.

The house of an important leader. The
thatch is of fine quality.

Left: A young man ready to go fishing. Fishermen often wear an eye-shade as a protection against the glare of the sun on the water. Right: A woman carrying a bowl of food as a contribution to a feast. She holds her child in a sling and shelters it with a mat of pandanus leaf.

The bride price at a wedding.

The ornamental palisade around a hamlet shrine in Nangali. In the background is the shrine of a warrior spirit decorated with skulls and other bones.

Introduction

FOR A SHORT PERIOD, IN 1942, the name Guadalcanal was on everybody's lips throughout the civilized world. This was when American Marines landed and, after much heavy fighting, stopped the Japanese advance into the southern Pacific. Until then the island had been of little importance to anyone save the 15,000 native Melanesian inhabitants. For half a century these folk had been in the nominal care of the Government of the Solomon Islands Protectorate, a dependency whose revenues were so meagre that full administrative control could not be established till 1927.

The Solomons as a whole are the peaks of a double chain of submerged mountains extending in a southeasterly direction from New Guinea. The two islands in the extreme northwest, Buka and Bougainville, are Australian territory, but the remainder are British. The chief islands are Choiseul, New Georgia, Ysabel, Guadalcanal, Florida, Malaita, and San Cristoval. There are numerous volcanoes, and violent earthquakes frequently occur.

Guadalcanal—sometimes spelt Guadalcanar—is about 85 miles long and, at its widest, 30 broad. Next to Bougainville it is the largest island of the archipelago. A ridge running along the southern coast reaches a height of over 8000 feet (Mount Popomanasiu), but the northern portion is a gently sloping plain. At the western end the foothills rise directly from the sea, and in the east they approach to within a couple of miles of it. The climate is hot and wet, dominated half the year by the southeast trade wind and the other half by the northwest monsoon.

The people are dark brown in color, clean limbed, and of medium stature: the average height for an adult male is just over 5 feet 6 inches, though a few individuals are much taller. Their heads are long and narrow, and many are slightly prognathous. The women crop their hair, but the men allow theirs to grow into a fuzzy mop. In earlier times both sexes went naked until puberty. At this age the youths donned a pubic band made from either a leaf of pandanus palm or a strip of bark cloth and kept in place by a string around the waist. At first the girls wore a fringe in front, but after marriage they replaced this with a short skirt of dried banana leaves or fiber. Today the usual garment for the men is a loincloth of calico, supplemented on special occasions with a shirt. The women still stick to the old skirts, though a number like to cover it with a cotton frill.

My first visit to Guadalcanal took place in 1927, my latest in 1945. I was there several times in the intervening years and in this book shall mainly present results from a study carried out in the northeastern district during 1933. For convenience I shall use the present tense when discussing conditions as they were then.

The natives with whom I worked do not distinguish themselves as a group from their neighbors, though they practice the same set of customs and speak a unique dialect, referred to, after one of the larger rivers, as *Kaoka* (miscalled by Europeans *Kaukau*).[1] Further west along the plain the customs are similar despite a change of language; in the interior both customs and language differ; and in the east, at the tip of the island, there is a third body of customs and still another language.

The Kaoka-speakers are spread over five politically autonomous villages: Mbambasu on the coast to the east; then Longgu, also on the coast; then Nangali, 3 or 4 miles inland; and finally Mboli and Paupau, both on the coast. I lived in Longgu, but stayed for some time in each of the other communities.

At the outset the people thought it odd that a European without some special ax to grind should want to take up residence in a native house and spend his time learning the language and endlessly discussing their doings and beliefs. Unlike the officers of the administration, I was indifferent about whether or not they obeyed the newly imposed laws; unlike the missionaries, I never condemned pagan ceremonies; unlike the planters, I had no need of laborers; and unlike the traders, I had nothing to sell. But after a month or two my presence everywhere, with notebooks and camera, came to be taken for granted. My neighbors even made me their regular confidant. So closely were they linked to their fellows that it was unwise for them to discuss their vexations openly with one another; but they welcomed the opportunity to unburden themselves to a sympathetic and understanding outsider behind closed doors. It might be said that I arrived at a knowledge of the anatomy of the society by diligent effort but that I mastered its physiology—the way in which things actually functioned—by patiently listening to unsolicited outpourings.

The settlements have the same appearance they had when Europeans first arrived. All the buildings rest directly on the ground and are of identical general design, though some are better constructed than others. The walls are made from saplings split in half and lashed firmly with stout creeper between pairs of uprights, and the roof is thatched with leaves of the ivory-nut palm, a species of sago. Small pebbles or shingles from the beach serve instead of flooring, and the end of the dwelling where people sleep is covered with coconut-leaf mats. The doorways have a high sill to prevent the entry of village

---

[1] See W. G. Ivens, 1934, pp. 601 to 621; and 1937, pp. 165 to 193. Both papers are based on a translation of parts of the Church of England *Book of Common Prayer*.

At present, Solomon-Island pidgin English (which differs somewhat from the better known New-Guinea pidgin English) serves as a lingua franca. This is a speech that the islanders have themselves developed. The vocabulary is largely derived from English, the grammar and pronunciation from the local dialects.

Note on the pronunciation of native words. Vowels are pronounced as in Italian, consonants as in English: *ng* as in "singer"; *ngg* as the ng in "finger." The apostrophe (for example, in *sa'i* and *pe'o*) represents a glottal stop.

pigs, and the door itself is cut from a single slab of wood. There are no windows, and the interior of the house is dark even at noon.

Today some of the people are Christians. Of these the majority belong to the Church of England, and all five villages have an Anglican church, in which services are conducted by resident catechists—natives from the neighboring island of Florida (sometimes called *Nggela* or *Gela*)—who also run the schools. In Longgu there are two additional churches, one for the few Baptists and another for the half-a-dozen Roman Catholics.

Like most Melanesians, the villagers are horticulturalists. Their principal crop is the yam, with taro, sweet potatoes, and bananas as subsidiaries. Steel axes and knives have replaced the old stone implements, but the chief gardening tool remains the digging stick, a stout pole with one end sharpened to a point.

Other vegetable foods include coconuts, Canarium almonds, breadfruit, and various other fruits. The coconut palms are planted in groves around the villages, and almond and breadfruit trees in the bush. A quantity of tobacco is also grown for pipe smoking; in addition each householder owns a patch of areca palms and pepper vines to provide two of the ingredients for the betel-nut mixture that everybody chews. (The third ingredient is lime, obtained by burning blocks of dried coral.)

Sea foods furnish the bulk of the protein in the diet. The women collect mussels, green snails, clams, and crustacea on the reef; the men catch fish from canoes or from the shore, using spears, lines, and nets. In most parts of the Pacific canoes are constructed with an outrigger, but on Guadalcanal, as on all the large islands of the Solomon group (and on some of those of the Bismarck Archipelago to the north), the side float is missing. The craft are here built of planks sewn together and caulked with natural gum. In former times the people paddled their canoes and did not employ a sail.

Pork is also highly valued, and every married man has a herd of domestic pigs, which he or his wife feeds each evening. The meat is reserved for ceremonial occasions, and he kills an animal only when he wishes to hold a feast, as, for example, at a wedding or a funeral. At such times the guests may gorge themselves until they are ill. A few men are skilled in hunting wild pigs, but the amount of game contributed to the supplies of the total village population is minimal.

A European-owned coconut plantation is located between Mbambasu and Longgu, and west of Paupau there are several such plantations. The youths sign on as indentured wage laborers at these plantations, where they spend about six years. They return home at the age of twenty-two or so, when they are ready for marriage.[2] Rations, tobacco, soap, clothing, and bedding are provided, and the cash earnings—in 1933 a minimum of 2 dollars and 80 cents (1 pound sterling) per month—serve to pay taxes and to buy various goods of Western manufacture now considered to be essential, such as steel tools, simple cotton clothing, and household utensils of all kinds.

---

[2] The natives do not count the passing years, and nobody is aware of how old he is. My statements about people's ages here and later in the book are therefore to be regarded as guesses.

1

Social Structure

THE KAOKA-SPEAKERS, together with the natives from the adjoining strip of coast as far west as Point Cruz, a distance of nearly 50 miles, are divided into five matrilineal dispersed clans named Hambata, Lasi, Naokama, Thimbo, and Thonggo, respectively. (There is no word in Kaoka for clan, but *tautauva* means fellow clansman; *tautauva nau,* my clansman, my clansmen; *tautauva mama nau,* my father's clansman, my father's clansmen.) These terms reputedly date back to the founder of the Guadalcanal social systems, the culture heroine Koevasi, who is credited with molding the first human being. This person, a woman, gave birth successively to five sons and five daughters. She married them off in pairs, and every wife became the ancestress of a separate clan. Koevasi also decreed that the pattern of lines on a child's right hand would be derived from the mother and thus give proof of group membership, whereas that on the left hand would mirror the father's right hand and hence establish paternity. (Yet people from all the clans who examined my palms all claimed me as a fellow clan member.)

Persons belonging to the same clan accept a number of mutual obligations "because of the flesh and blood." A householder offers hospitality to travelers belonging to his clan, and, in earlier times, clansmen from opposing bands of warriors who found themselves face to face in battle turned aside to look for somebody else to fight.

Clans are identified with two bird totems and one fish totem: *manu ambu* and *i'ia ambu; manu* is the word for bird, *i'ia* for fish, and *ambu* for taboo, sacred, set apart. It is said that in olden days travelers and warriors decorated themselves with the feathers of their clan birds in order to be easily recognizable, but today neither birds nor fish are of any significance. People assert that they avoid the flesh of their bird totems, but as no bird is at any time eaten, the statement has little meaning. The totem fish, too, are so seldom caught that during the many months I spent on the island no one was able to point them out. The only time I heard a totem mentioned in general conversation was

4

when a man announced that because he had dreamed of a parakeet (a bird of Naokama) the previous night, he supposed that the Naokama wife of a cousin living in Nangali must have conceived.

Sexual affairs within the clan are frowned upon, and marriage is supposed to be "unthinkable," though I recorded a couple of recent cases when this took place within the clan. A girl had become pregnant by a young man from her own unit, and the parents decided that clan incest was preferable to illegitimacy. The rest of the people expressed profound disgust, but they took no positive action against the pair. The other affair had a similar background.

The chief importance of the clan organization is its application to land rights. The river deltas, where the recurring floods would destroy boundary marks, are treated as common property,[1] but the rest of the land is cut into named blocks of varying acreage, some 2 or 3, others 50 or 60 acres large. These are grouped into series, each of which is bound up with a clan. In and around Longgu village are hundreds of Hambata blocks, hundreds of Lasi blocks, and so on. By virtue of his birth into a clan, an individual acquires the inalienable right to select sites for his house and cultivations on the territory of that clan. A Hambata man can erect a dwelling on any Hambata village block and plant his yams and coconuts on any Hambata agricultural block, a Lasi man erect his dwelling on any Lasi village block and plant his yams and coconuts on any Lasi agricultural block. A Hambata father may invite his son, necessarily from a different clan—indeed, he is free to invite any of his kinsmen or affines—to use a Hambata building or gardening plot, and, unless a serious quarrel occurred, nobody would dream of challenging the young man as an intruder or demand his withdrawal; yet he is permitted to be there as a favor and is to some degree an outsider. Dismissal for misbehavior is always a possibility, and it would also be a breach of etiquette for the son to issue a further invitation to his son on the same terms as a Hambata clansman.

The clan system is reflected in religion. Each group has three great spirits —a warrior, a shark, and a snake—to which the members offer sacrifices.

The Village

The average settlement has a population of 175 to 200, and the residents, unlike clansmen, can always give exact details of how they are related to one another. Marriage within the community is common, and villagers are often united in two or three ways as different sorts of cousins. In these circumstances they select the tie that is appropriate to their age. Even the few men who, in fact, are strangers have become incorporated into the framework. These are mostly ex-laborers who served their term of employment on a nearby

---

[1] In May 1933, after three days of incessant rain, the Simiu River, on the outskirts of Longgu, changed its course and carried twenty gardens into the sea.

plantation. During his employment, each of them had become friendly with a local villager who, on the completion of the contract of service, had adopted him as a brother and undertaken to find him a wife. Other people had signified their acceptance of him by working out pseudokinship ties.

There is no absolute rule that bridegroom and bride must come from the same place, and intervillage unions occur. In the past the leaders of friendly communities reaffirmed strategic alliances by arranging for their respective dependents to be affianced to one another. It follows that, although few people are closely related to all the inhabitants of the surrounding villages, everybody has some near kinsmen outside his own area.

Land, as I mentioned, appertains to the clan. As the same time, the residents of a village exploit only the clan territories of their own locality. All the gardens of the Longgu folk are located within a semicircle having a radius of about 2 miles (the coast forms the diameter), and here not one person from Nangali or Mbambasu cultivates a plot. The river deltas are exceptional. as was indicated. These belong to the entire village, and householders, regardless of their clan affiliation, choose any patch they fancy.

Rarely does the village become an isolated unit of economic cooperation. Few tasks demand the presence of large numbers of workers, and for most of those that do, such as housebuilding, the man who needs the help calls on the full quota of his relatives and affines, those from nearby as well as more distant places. A separate village labor force comes into being only when certain feasts are held and when such activities as trading expeditions have to be arranged. The feasts are conceived as enhancing the reputation of the full community; and, till recently, several canoes took part in an overseas voyage to ensure the presence of sufficient men to put up a defense in case unfavorable currents drove the fleet to some hostile shore.

In the juridical and political spheres the situation is rather different. On the one hand, the village is the largest body within which regular institutions exist for maintaining order and settling disputes; and, on the other, it is the smallest war-making group. Each settlement has a headman, one of whose principal jobs is to call the seniors to a meeting when any matter of importance has to be decided. At times this assembly resembles a court, as when it investigates charges of wrongdoing, and at times it is more like a committee or a parliament, as when it deals with such policy questions as whether an attack is to be carried out against some enemy.

As with the clan, the unity of the village is carried over into religion. In theory, when approaching the great spirits householders ought to confine themselves to the worship of those of their own clan; in practice there is a strong tendency for them to follow the headman and to look to the great spirits of his clan. The office is not hereditary, and when a leader has died the ablest of the remaining seniors takes over. So if a Hambata headman is followed by one from Thonggo, then interest in the Hambata spirits is for the time being replaced by a concentration on those of Thonggo.

The Hamlet

The villages are made up of several distinct hamlets separated from one another by stretches of bush. In the coast settlements the hamlets are strung along the main pathway like beads on a string, and in Nangali they lie within of curves of a shallow winding river. The largest consist of about ten houses, the smallest of four or five.

Each hamlet is located on a block of clan land and takes the name by which this area is known. (A few villages, including Longgu, are named after a particular hamlet, allegedly because this was where the first houses were built.) Most of the male residents who are apparently over the age of thirty, and some who are a year or two younger, belong to the same clan. In Longgu village, progressing from west to east, the majority of the senior householders from Longgu hamlet are of Naokama clan, those from Kioramo hamlet of Thimbo clan, those from Olombau hamlet of Thimbo clan, those from Mbokola hamlet of Thonggo clan, those from Totongo hamlet of Lasi clan, and so on. Individuals of a clan who live together in a hamlet are referred to by an expression meaning literally "separate headwaters" or "separate sources" and hence "tributary" (*ouvusi mbouni-wai*), and people explain that just as different streams flowing together become a broad river, so different tributary groups coalesce to form a clan. The appropriate English term is subclan—though this implies one of several parts cut from something that is complete instead of the native notion of separate pieces that can form a collection. Usually most of the members of the subclan are descended from a known ancestress, but there is no feeling that this must be the case.

These localized clan sectors come into being in the following way. A boy grows up in his father's household and forms a strong attachment to him and to the men next door. When in early manhood he marries, he builds a house for himself and his wife in this hamlet. Buildings, however, unless very stoutly constructed, soon fall into ruins, and within five or six years he must think of a new dwelling. Generally by then he has a young family to support and realizes that the rights derived from the clan, especially those relating to land, are of greater significance than the favors he enjoys as a father's son. Accordingly, the chances are that he will move to clan territory. If his maternal uncles are resident in the village, as often happens, he usually joins them. They will have taken at least as much interest in him as his paternal uncles have taken; they will have taught him all about his clan and what membership in it means, and pointed out that when they die he and certain other relatives (his brothers and the sons of his mother's sisters) will inherit the personal property. It is true that the canoes, some of the trees, and many household effects will have to be destroyed during the funeral—as well as the garden produce, pigs, and half the valuables distributed at the subsequent feast—but what remains is still likely to be of value.

If the young man's mother came from another village any of three possible courses of action is open to him. He may pick out one of the hamlets of his clan from within the settlement, he and his brothers may found a new hamlet, or he may leave his place of birth and take up permanent residence in the village of his mother's brothers.

The situation in Guadalcanal may be contrasted with that in the Trobriands, home of the best-documented matrilineal people of Melanesia.[2] A Trobriand lad leaves his parents much earlier, at about the age of puberty. We shall see why this is so in the next section.

A woman sometimes asserts that because her children tend to replenish the subclan of her brothers, she also belongs to the group. But although she and the brothers frequently visit one another, her husband's subclan hamlet is her home, and her chief loyalty is to him. In theory her skull has its final resting place in her brothers' shrine, but, in practice, the husband more often than not claims it for his shrine.

The people of the hamlet, with the subclan as a core, form a social, economic, and religious unit. One of the houses, though externally identical with the rest, serves as a club. Here the menfolk gather during the late afternoon, and later, when the evening meal is over, the youths and old men return to spend the night. The women use the spring where they fill the water bottles as a similar meeting place. They gather here for a chat and occasionally, in order to continue their socializing, pool their supplies and cook together. Gardening is also a hamlet affair, although guests may frequently be present. The men combine to clear a big patch of clan ground, which they then divide into allotments, one for each household. A wife looks after her own family plots, but she and the other women carry out the various tasks simultaneously and are within easy reach of one another when the time comes for a rest or a snack. The men take a large canoe and go fishing together, and every few days the women make up a party to gather clams and snails on the reef. Finally, there are hamlet shrines where the ancestors of the subclan receive sacrifices.

The Household

The household consists of a group of people who share a dwelling: a man, his wife, their unmarried children, and possibly a few extra persons, such as the man's elderly parents or parents-in-law, an unmarried sister or sister-in-law, or an orphaned nephew or niece.

The father is head of the household and exercises full domestic authority. He has the right to tell the rest what work they should do and, if they are younger than himself, to scold or punish them for disobedience. But he has corresponding obligations. He must see that all his dependents are adequately fed, clothed, and provided with sufficient wealth to meet their ceremonial com-

---

[2] See B. Malinowski, 1922, 1926, 1929, 1935; E. R. Leach, 1958; M. S. Robinson, 1962; and J. P. Singh Uberoi, 1962.

mitments. In practice he delegates command in certain spheres to his wife. She harvests the crops and is responsible for preparing, cooking, and serving the everyday meals. He therefore permits her a free hand in all matters relating to the hearth.

Clearing and fencing, as pointed out, are done by the hamlet residents in collaboration with their guests. But the actual gardening is performed by and for the household. Each family has its own plots, and it is the man's job to plant the seed yams and place the stakes for the yam vines, and the woman's job to keep the beds free from weeds. The produce is subsequently gathered in and becomes household property. The members feed upon it and use it, by favor of the head of the house, to make appropriate presentations in fulfillment of their various social responsibilities. The pigs, fish, shell fish, and other supplies also pass into the household commissariat.

The man's dependents, except perhaps when his father or father-in-law is included, are looked upon, in the jural sense, as minors. He takes action when one of them is wronged and pays the compensation should they be guilty of misconduct.

The reason for the late development of the close tie between uterine nephew and maternal uncle will now be plain. In the Trobriand Islands a man supports his sisters and their children, and at harvest sends large quantities of yams to replenish the storehouses of his brothers-in-law.[3] As a consequence, he feels at liberty to interfere in the running of their household concerns, and the children are from the beginning instructed to treat him as their most important relative. According to one authority, the father is in some respects a background figure: more an affine—the mother's husband—than a true kinsman.[4]

Structure and Organization

In my *Kinship and Marriage in a New Guinea Village* I classified Melanesian societies according to their structural differences.[5] One set of communities is built on a single localized patrilineal or matrilineal clan or subclan, another on several localized patrilineal or matrilineal clans or subclans, and in still another set unilineal groupings are not found.[6] In societies of the first type the spouse, because of the rule of clan exogamy, must always be sought outside; in those of the second type the spouse can, and frequently does, come from inside the settlement; and in those of the third type, since marriage between all first cousins (and sometimes all second cousins as well) is forbidden, the spouse usually comes from a distant region. Factors of this kind have a direct bearing on village solidarity and antagonisms.

---

[3] B. Malinowski, 1935, Vol. I, Chap. 6.

[4] E. R. Leach, 1961, pp. 1 to 27. But it should be noted that M. S. Robinson, 1962, after examining the same information as Leach, came to different conclusions.

[5] H. I. Hogbin, 1963, pp. 31 to 34.

[6] There are also a few societies with two distinct sets of groupings: membership in the one group will depend on unilineal descent, membership in the other on choice.

The Guadalcanal material poses the problem of how the day-to-day organization is affected. In societies with patrilineal descent, whether there is one group or many, a man generally spends his life near his brothers, father, paternal uncles, and paternal uncles' sons; in societies with matrilineal descent, at a certain stage a man and his brothers generally move to be with their maternal uncles' and maternal aunts' sons; and in societies without unilineal groups, he can choose, though only within certain limits. The result is that, for the sake of convenience if nothing else, the smaller working gangs tend to be made up respectively of the patrilineal kin, the matrilineal kin, and kin of different kinds. But important tasks demand more helpers, and for some undertakings a man is grateful for the assistance of a wide circle of kinsfolk and affines. The group of men engaged in housebuilding, canoe construction, or weaving the large fishing nets has therefore much the same composition everywhere, regardless of the structural framework. The only qualification is that unilineal descent may create a slight bias. A man from a patrilineal society is perhaps likely to consider that, although his firmest bonds are with his clan fellows, he is a little closer to his mother's clansmen than to his other relatives; and, correspondingly, a man from a matrilineal society is perhaps likely to consider that, although his firmest bonds also are with his clan fellows, he is a little closer to his father's clansmen than to his other relatives.

૪ ▫ Kinship Terms and Behavior

The terms are mainly reserved for reference: they are regularly used in address only by young children to their parents, uncles, and aunts and by men to their sisters' sons and daughters. The sole occasion on which I heard them otherwise used in speaking to someone, was when an oblique reminder had to be made of obligations as yet unfulfilled or forgotten. "Ah, brother, I see you have been busy," said one of my neighbors when the person in question had failed to help him repair the thatch of his house.

Two types of terms can be distinguished: those that incorporate a special kind of possessive pronoun and those that do not. The former designate the abstract relationship by the form incorporating the third personal pronoun, as in these examples: *nggale-nggu,* my son, *nggale-mu,* thy son, *nggale-na,* his son, son. The terms of the other type can stand alone: *sa'i,* maternal uncle, *sa'i nau,* my maternal uncle, *sa'i 'oe,* thy maternal uncle, and *sa'i ingaia,* his maternal uncle. I cannot offer any explanation for the difference.

PARENTS AND CHILDREN   Parents are responsible for the nourishment, early upbringing, and training of their offspring. They have the right of punishment to enforce obedience but in practice seldom administer severe thrashings.

Bonds between the members of the family are strong and enduring. Although the father cannot give away rights to clan land, he frequently invites his sons to make gardens there, and he may also hand a certain amount of wealth to them, though the major portion must go to the uterine nephews. The rule of matrilineal inheritance applies less strictly to magical knowledge, and he teaches most of his spells to his sons.

The children are equally devoted, and ultimately, when the elderly couple can no longer look after themselves properly, a son or a daughter may take them into his or her household. By now the right of punishment is reversed, and sons may hit a troublesome father or mother without incurring serious public censure. Yet very few of them ever do so.

The measure of filial affection may be gathered from the man's postponement of his removal to a hamlet of his own clan till after the birth of children, when he is approaching the age of thirty. If he is the youngest of several brothers he may wait till after the old man's death.

The theory of conception mirrors—and validates—customary practices. As a rule matrilineal descent goes hand in hand with the belief that the mother is alone responsible for the embryo in her womb. Here in Guadalcanal it is thought that the flesh comes from her, through the dammed up blood; the father, by supplying the semen, is held to be the creator of the skeletal structure. We saw that each person supposedly carries the marks of his father's clan on the palm of his left hand. It often happens, too, that a man asked which is his clan gives the correct answer and then adds, "begotten by Such-and-such," naming the group of his father. Again, the common justification of the minority who stay on in the father's hamlet is, "He made my bones; I stand up because of him."

The word for "father" is *mama,* for "mother" *tike,* and for "son" or "daughter" *nggale-na.*

BROTHERS AND SISTERS   Brothers grow up in the one household and share numerous rights and privileges. They are nearly on an equal footing, though the elder enjoys a slight superiority and can give orders to the younger, who should obey and refrain from answering back. Each can depend upon the other for all manner of help, and, despite the fact that their close association sometimes leads them to quarrel, the differences are seldom of long duration. The first-born may revile his juniors today and next week work alongside them as though nothing untoward had taken place. To keep trouble to a minimum, they mostly take the precaution when migrating to the hamlet of their clan to place their dwellings at some distance from one another.

Sisters also cherish a warm mutual regard. The eldest acts as a substitute in the event of the mother's death, and, in theory, she can direct the activities of the rest. But after marriage each sister joins her husband, and so they must separate. If they have to live in different settlements, common interests and sympathy are kept up by frequent visits and exchanges of small gifts of food.

Brothers and sisters have similar feelings. They avoid ribald jokes and bad language in one another's presence but otherwise have few reserves. They sit in the house together, chat freely, and have no compunction about eating from the same platter. A youth who has been out in the rain may casually ask his sister to give him some dry clothing, and he thinks nothing of changing in her presence, though he turns away to do so. He does not go near a beach or pool when aware that she is bathing there, but if he comes across her by accident neither feels embarrassed.

A man is prepared to bring his young sister into his household should their parents die; when married, she may take temporary refuge with him if her husband beats her. The brother may urge her to return, but not until he is sure that she will be well received. The sister also visits her brother and brings him small gifts of food from herself and her husband. She is quick to be at hand should he be taken ill, when she rushes to prepare delicacies and help his wife with the nursing.

A man refers to his elder brother, and a woman to her elder sister, as *to'o-na;* a man to his younger brother, and a woman to her younger sister, as *si-na;* and a man to his sister, and a woman to her brother, as *vavune-na.*

UNCLES AND AUNTS   The father's brothers behave in much the same way as he does. They live nearby and play with the child and take it home to meals. Later they help the parents teach the child the proper way to behave and how to carry out various tasks. The child in turn treats them as secondary fathers.

Similarly, the father's and the mother's sisters act as though they were mothers and in return are treated as such, except for some diminution of affection.

The "father" term *mama* is applied to his brothers and, by courtesy, to the husbands of his sisters and to the husbands of the mother's sisters; and the "mother" term *tike* is applied to the father's and the mother's sisters and, by courtesy, to the wives of the father's brothers. All these people refer to their nephews and nieces by the term for son and daughter, *nggale-na.*

The mother's brothers are in a special category. In the beginning their demeanor resembles that of the paternal uncles, but by the time the child reaches puberty, especially if he is a boy, they start explaining about the clan and its accompanying rights and responsibilities. They also have a special interest in the child's conduct and therefore actively support the father's efforts to secure discipline. A youth of twenty is always prepared to agree that his maternal uncles are the most important relatives after his father (not, as in the Trobriands, that they are more important than the father).

The word for "mother's brother" and also for "sister's child" is *sa'i.* The wife of the mother's brother is referred to as a courtesy by the "mother" term, *tike.*

COUSINS   The father's brothers' children and the mother's sisters' children (the parallel cousins) are treated like brothers and sisters and referred to by the same terms, *to'o-na, si-na,* and *vavune-na.* (*To'o-na,* older brother or older male cousin of a man and older sister or older female cousin of a woman, and *si-na,* younger brother or younger male cousin of a man and younger sister or younger female cousin of a woman, are applied on the basis of absolute age, not seniority of descent line.) In early life a boy is generally more intimate with the children of his father's brothers. He spends his childhood in the same hamlet and plays with them daily, and in adolescence and early manhood he carries out much of his work in their company. He and the children of his mother's sisters, however, belong to the one clan. At first he may meet them only occasionally, as when his mother calls upon her sisters or these women invite him to stay; but at the age of about thirty he becomes their neighbor within a subclan group and collaborates with them most of the time.

The father's sisters' children and the mother's brothers' children (the cross-cousins) are also treated like brothers and sisters. Although they do not occupy a hamlet together—except perhaps temporarily when a man moves to his maternal uncles' place before all the maternal uncles' sons have departed—they are expected to be at all times loyal and helpful. But it is also imperative that they show one another the outward forms of mutual respect. They may use personal names but not indulge in joking or loose talk; they may eat in the same gathering, provided each has a separate platter; and they may sleep under one roof if they take the trouble to erect a dividing curtain or screen. If a man should inadvertently speak of sexual matters within earshot of the son or daughter of a father's sister or a mother's brother, or should he be hungry and take their food, or come upon such a person naked, either asleep or awake, he would have to hand over valuables to hide his shame.

The natives offer no explanation for the restrictions. In this respect they are unlike the people of certain other Melanesian communities in which rights to property are dependent on a system of matrilineal groups. The Busama of New Guinea maintain that their similar taboos are specifically designed to preserve harmony in a situation fraught with difficulty. The son, they say, is hindered from displaying anger at being forced to vacate his father's ground in favor of the father's sisters' sons.[7] We cannot hope to know whether, in fact, a conscious purpose lies behind the custom, but may agree about the effect. The societies of Guadalcanal, however, have an added complication to face. In Busama, land tenure alone is bound up with group membership, and a man is free to bequeath his personal possessions to his sons. By contrast, the Guadalcanal rule, while permitting the householder during his lifetime to give "a few" of his goods—precise amount unspecified—to his son, insists that at death everything must go to the sisters' sons. Should these latter then suspect their cousin of robbing them of part of their inheritance, the rising tide of annoyance at the loss may, for the time being, obliterate their sense of decorum. At some of the funerals I attended the heirs openly accused the dead man's son of theft, and once they would have attacked him with spears in the presence of the still-unburied corpse had not bystanders rushed in and pointed out the enormity of their offense.

Sexual relations between a man and a father's sister's, or a mother's brother's daughter, despite the fact that she belongs to a different clan from his, are regarded as even more reprehensible than affairs within the clan; marriage between such persons is not only out of the question but has never taken place. Several reasons are given. First, the daughter of the father's sister is the flesh

[7] H. I. Hogbin, 1963, p. 93.

of her mother, just as the daughter of the mother's brother is the bone of her father. To conduct a liaison with either of the girls would therefore be disrespectful to the aunt or the uncle. If fornication nevertheless occurred and was discovered the aunt or uncle would be vexed and hence unwilling to discharge the responsibilities proper to the relationship. Marriage is ruled out partly because of the incompatibility of the behavior required of, on the one hand, aunts and uncles and, on the other, parents-in-law, and partly because of the conventions about bride price. It is argued that a ridiculous situation would be created if the same person were expected to contribute because of his ties with the bridegroom and also demand a share on account of his ties with the bride. Again, it is impossible to say whether the taboos were deliberately designed to remove the possibility of sexual relations or marriage between cousins of this type, but their effect is certainly to prevent intimacy.

A person refers to his father's sisters' children and his mother's brothers' children by the term *ula-na*.

OTHER RELATIVES   The only remaining term for cognates is *vua*, which means "grandparent" and "grandchild." The old folk are indulgent to the youngsters, and the youngsters have a great fondness for the old folk.

The nine terms are applied to all the other cognates. Persons of the grandparent and of the grandchild generations to whom a genealogical connection can be traced are called, like them, *vua;* males of the parent generation on the father's side to whom a genealogical connection can be traced are called, like him, *mama;* females of the parent generation on both sides to whom a genealogical connection can be traced are called, like the mother, *tike;* males of the parent generation on the mother's side to whom a genealogical connection can be traced are called, like the maternal uncle, *sa'i;* persons of the same generation as the speaker on the father's side to whom a genealogical connection can be traced through a male, and persons of the same generation as the speaker on the mother's side to whom a genealogical connection can be traced through a female, are called, like the brothers and sisters, *to'o-na, si-na,* and *vavune-na;* persons of the same generation as the speaker on the father's side to whom a genealogical connection can be traced through a female, and persons of the same generation as the speaker on the mother's side to whom a genealogical connection can be traced through a male, are called, like the father's sisters' children and the mother's brothers' children, *ula-na;* if a female is speaking, all persons of the child generation to whom a genealogical connection can be traced are called, like the son and daughter, *nggale-na;* if a male is speaking, the offspring of all males of his generation to whom a genealogical connection can be traced are called, like the son and daughter, *nggale-na;* and, if a male is speaking, the offspring of all females of his generation to whom a genealogical connection can be traced are called, like the sisters' children, *sa'i.* Behavior is roughly comparable, and everybody referred to as *mama,* for instance, conducts himself in some degree like the real father and is treated in some degree as though he were. This applies particularly to people who are in frequent contact, such as the residents of a village.

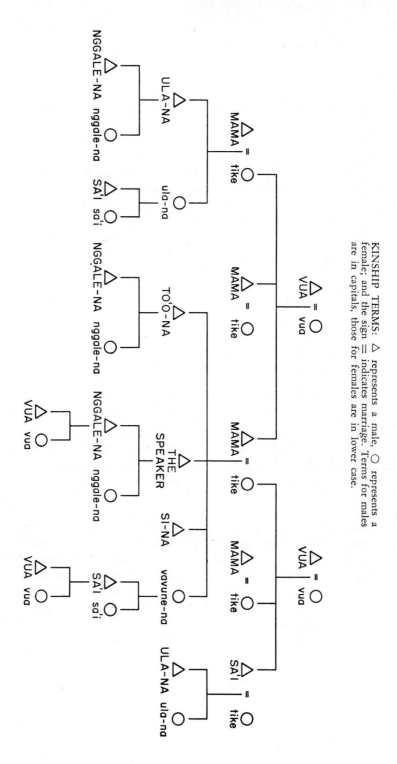

KINSHIP TERMS: △ represents a male, ○ represents a female; and the sign = indicates marriage. Terms for males are in capitals, those for females are in lower case.

A Comparison with the Hill People

Before settling in Longgu I made a short tour of the interior and became acquainted with a number of natives who later, on their visits to the seaboard for trade and other purposes, paid calls on me and answered my questions. I was able to gain some knowledge of the local customs, and this final section of the chapter will give a brief account of the social structure. The material is of general interest in that it highlights the remarkable diversity in the types of Melanesian kinship organization. Thus, on the one island of Guadalcanal there is the matrilineal moiety and multiclan system I am now about to describe (found in the interior and on the south coast), the system of five matrilineal clans (the north coast from Mbambasu to Point Cruz), the system of four matrilineal clans (the north-west corner[8]), the system of three matrilineal clans (the west coast around Wanderer Bay), and the system without unilineal groupings of any kind (the east coast at Marau Sound, populated many generations ago, according to tradition, by settlers from Malaita). The variations are the more extraordinary in the face of the basic similarities in the spheres of economics and politics, not only in the Solomons but also throughout coastal New Guinea, the Bismarck Archipelago, and the New Hebrides. Suggested explanations include mass migrations, growth of population, and volcanic eruptions; but these remain no more than unsubstantiated speculations.[9]

The primary division is a pair of exogamous matrilineal moieties (*rau*) called Eagle and Hawk (*Manu-lava* and *Manu-kiki*—*manu*, bird, *lava*, big, *kiki*, small); the Eagle moiety is sometimes referred to as *Haravu*. The myth accounting for the grouping relates that Guadalcanal was built up from the seabed by the two men, Tzatza and Tzili, who, when they had finished, planted a fig tree and a Cordyline shrub (*sambaha* and *tzili*). An eagle perched on the fig, still the tallest of the forest trees, and laid two eggs, from which sprang a youth and a girl. Simultaneously two leaves fell to the ground from the Cordyline and changed into another youth and girl. The eagle girl married the Cordyline boy, thus founding the Eagle moiety, and the Cordyline girl married the eagle boy, thus founding the Hawk moiety. Subsequently, a sky spirit, Sivotohu, let down a vine to which he had attached pigs and all the other foodstuffs. The vine broke, and the end coiled across the land thereby causing the mountains and the rivers to appear. One piece of the vine turned into stone, which may be seen as a rocky outcrop to this day. Even now, so it is believed, a man's affiliation can be told from his temperament, his gait, and the way he holds himself. (I was claimed by each of the groups.)

The moieties are made up of scores of matrilineal clans (*raundake-ndake*), all bearing the names of different species of smaller birds.

The countryside consists of these clan districts, each of which is upwards

---

[8] W. H. R. Rivers, 1914, Vol. I, p. 243, gave six clans, but two of them, if they ever existed—and Rivers was relying on hearsay information—must long ago have disappeared.

[9] H. I. Hogbin, 1963, pp. 31 to 37.

of a square mile in area, and no piece of ground is unowned. Nowadays the Government officers insist on the establishment of villages, and there is one for every district. But most of the time such places are deserted, and the residents continue to live, as formerly, in isolated homesteads.

At marriage the bride leaves her parents and joins her husband. The sons, when they grow up, are allowed to erect a dwelling in their father's district, though only as a privilege. Many of them therefore migrate in early manhood to the district of their own clan, where their rights cannot be contested. Yet it is a fact that here in the interior the male members of a clan tend to be more widely dispersed than the male members of a subclan on the coast. An additional factor making for heterogeneity of district composition is that a prominent leader attracts as followers other relatives besides his uterine kinsmen.

The mother's brother is stated to be the most important of the relatives. It is agreed that he would be unlikely to kill his sisters' sons, but if ever this happened there would be no possibility of anyone's punishing him. His nephews must never sleep under his roof, and when walking along the same pathway they have to follow behind him.

Compared with the maternal uncle, the father is "just nothing"—"his sons need never obey him." At the same time, they have a strong attachment to him and are always deeply grieved when he dies.

Brother and sister are obliged to show mutual respect. A boy ceases to sleep in the family dwelling at the age of about ten and begins spending his nights in a club. From this time onward he and the girls of the family may never be alone together. Even in the presence of a crowd they keep their distance. A woman may cook food for her brother, but in no circumstances does she give it into his hands, and he never eats it in her company. The greatest insult, leading to instant bloodshed, is telling a man to eat his sister's excrement. If, however, he belongs to the opposite moiety, it is his own sister whom he feels obliged to kill. The insulter is then honor-bound to butcher his sister in turn.

Brothers also display reserve. They do not sleep in the same club unless a third party is on hand, and when eating they always have separate platters. Loose talk, including references to sex and excreta, are absolutely forbidden.

Cross-cousin marriage is permitted but not enjoined, and young people always show respect for their parents-in-law. The levirate is encouraged, and a young widower also prefers to marry a sister of his deceased wife.

The kinship terminology fails to distinguish cross-cousins, who necessarily belong to opposite moieties. They and parallel cousins are alike referred to by the words for brother and sister.[10] But, as in the Kaoka language, there is a special term, which is reciprocal, for maternal uncles and uterine nephews and nieces.

A person avoids addressing his brothers and sisters either by name or

---

[10] The fact that the Kaoka-speakers have special cross-cousin terms and no moieties, and their neighbors in the interior moieties and no special terms, may seem surprising. The question of consistency between social structure and kinship terminology is discussed in H. I. Hogbin, 1963, pp. 50 to 52.

by the kinship term. He even refrains from using words that have any resemblance to the names of his sisters. One man of my acquaintance whose sister was called Kolo, the expression for water, habitually referred to water as rain (*marambu*). A brother who finds it necessary to hail his sister calls out "Everybody!" or "Widow!" (*Kominiha!, Mantzona!*), and she, in a similar predicament, yells, "Son of So-and-so!" or "Father of Such-and-such!"

Kinship terms, not names, are appropriate in speaking to the parents, but mother's brothers and sisters' sons, as well as relatives-by-marriage, are barred from employing either terms or names. A person addressing his parent or child, his maternal uncle or uterine nephew, his parent-in-law or child-in-law has recourse to the dual form of the pronouns. He says to his father, for example, "May I go with the two of you to the garden?"

The terms are as follows: *kakua* or *tama-na*—father, father's brothers, father's sister's husband, mother's sister's husband; *kokoi* or *na-na*—mother, mother's sisters, father's sisters, father's brother's wife, mother's brother's wife; *tatai* or *vinda-na*—mother's brothers, sisters' children (man speaking); *kukua-na* —grandparents, grandchildren; *tokea*—older brothers (man speaking), older sisters (woman speaking); *kasi-na*—younger brothers (man speaking), younger sisters (woman speaking); *vavenge-na*—sisters (man speaking), brothers (woman speaking); *ndale-na*—children, brothers' children, sisters' children (woman speaking); *ati-na*—spouse; *iva-na*—brother's wife (man speaking), wife's sister, husband's brother; *kula-na*—sister's husband (woman speaking), husband's sister; *ndoma* or *lahi-na*—sister's husband (man speaking), wife's brother; *vungo-na*—parents-in-law, children-in-law. *Tokea* and *kasi-na* are also used for the wife's sister's husband and the husband's brother's wife; *vavenge-na* for the wife's brother's wife and the husband's sister's husband.

2

Sex and Marriage

CONSTANT REFERENCE will have to be made throughout this chapter to the local forms of ceremonial currency, and it will be convenient to say a word or two about them at the start. The most highly prized ceremonial currency consists of fathom-long strings of shell discs—white, pink, and deep red—fastened into sets of 12 (*talina*), 10 (*sausehe*), 8 (*matambala*), 6 (*malona*), and 4 (*konggana*). A single string is never cut, and the discs are only rethreaded when the cord has become frayed or has already snapped; but a man obliged to make contributions simultaneously to two relatives may break a set into its component strings in order to give some to each. Also valued are the canine teeth of dogs and the teeth of porpoises. A full unit of the currency is called a *ndovu*. This is a collection of a set of 12, of 10, of 8, of 6, and of 4 strings of discs, plus 40 dog's teeth and 100 porpoise teeth.

Prostitution

Children from the age of about seven play at weddings and at setting up house. The adults laugh tolerantly unless the boys begin "wanting to be real husbands" and lie down with the girls. The stock admonition then, even to youngsters of ten or eleven, is that females must have no physical contact with males till after marriage. Often somebody adds that brides ought to be virgins when they go to their husbands.

Till 1925, and possibly a little later, organized prostitution furnished the youths with an outlet for their sexual impulses and hence gave parents a measure of protection for older daughters. Several of the senior men had a harlot (*rembi*) attached to their households. Most of these were women who had been discovered in an intrigue, though a few were war captives.

Scandal damaged a girl's good name, and relatives had no hope of receiving the full bride price for her. To offset the loss the eldest of her maternal uncles had the right to take her away from the parents and sell her sexual favors. Generally he used her for the continuing enrichment of himself and his brothers, but sometimes, if he was of generous disposition, he preferred to hand her over to a headman from either his own or a neighboring village in return for the payment of a lump sum of about 4 *ndovu* (160 strings, 160 dog's teeth, and 400 porpoise teeth), roughly the equivalent of an ordinary bride price. He dismissed on the grounds of carelessness any claim that the girl's father put forward for a share and restricted his donations to the girl's matrilateral kin.

Some notion of what the manager of a prostitute expected may be gathered from the magic performed over her. He sought out a specialist, who rubbed a bespelled bundle of leaves—all selected for their distinctive coloring, aromatic scent, or irritant qualities—over her sleeping mats. One spell, freely translated, ran as follows:

She does not sit in the house,
She is ever restless, strolling up and down.
She itches all the time for men.
Sores do not afflict her, and her skin is without blemish.
Her skin shines and glows like a crimson Cordyline leaf in a dark forest.
Men look at her and think of copulation.
She belongs to no clan, she has no kinsfolk.
She arouses desire in the trees and in the stones.
She seeks men always, knowing not night from day.
She wants penis all the time.
She needs no sleep, she feels no shame.
She is like a bitch on heat, attracting dogs in the darkness and in the sunlight.
She does not wait or pause, she is always ready.
And the young men desire her also.
Yet her womb is closed, and she never conceives.
She is a tree without fruit.

The provision of a house for the prostitute was the responsibility of her manager, but she did no work, not even cooking. His family prepared her meals and carried them to her dwelling. To be provocative, she wore a short grass skirt and many ornaments; and she spent her spare time bathing and rubbing her limbs with fragrant oil.

The youths of her own subclan were expected to keep away, but otherwise the clan prohibition did not apply. The standard fee for someone from within the cluster of villages round about was 2 porpoise teeth. This the prostitute collected and later gave to her manager. But he also took her with him on overseas voyages, and from foreigners he made her ask 5 porpoise teeth. None of these valuables went to her father or to any patrilateral relative.

The prostitute did not continue her career indefinitely. After a few years, when pregnancy or the loss of first youthfulness reduced her earning power, the manager decided that he had better marry her off. Again he caused magic to be performed, this time to keep her true to her husband and abundantly fertile. She then took a ritual bath "to wash away the memory." The bride price, about a quarter of that expected for a girl with an unblemished record, went in the normal way to the patrilateral and matrilateral relatives.

It is said that former prostitutes were no more likely to carry on adulterous affairs than other wives and that most of them remained faithful for the rest of their lives. This statement my observations confirmed. I can also vouch for the fact that, "for shame's sake," other people avoided mentioning the past within the woman's hearing. People told me about prostitution in general terms within a few weeks of my arrival; they were angry at the Government's action in stamping out the custom, partly on account of the alleged present difficulty of preventing seductions, partly on account of the drying-up of a source of income. But I was in the place for months before anyone mentioned that four of the present housewives had been harlots; and then each speaker asked me to keep the information to myself. All the women are of good repute, and although two are married to Malaita settlers, men who had been laborers on a plantation nearby, and a third to a widower some fifteen years older than herself, the fourth is the honored spouse of the most important Longgu leader.

Seduction

How common premarital affairs are today is difficult to establish. Some men insist that all the girls are really promiscuous, but others condemn such statements as absurd. Why, if chastity is so rare, they ask, are scandals infrequent? I am inclined to accept the latter point of view. Privacy is difficult to attain in a small community where people are always passionately interested in the doings of their neighbors; moreover, in Guadalcanal, parents take the greatest care to arrange that unmarried daughters shall be continually accompanied, if only by a child, while away from home. Should a boy and girl known to have an interest in each other be discovered missing, at once suspicions are aroused and the couple are watched. It is possibly significant also that girls are said to engage in homosexual practices specifically "because the youths are forbidden"—and no one condemns them for it. (Yet the elders strongly disapprove of the common habit of mutual masturbation among the males.)

The normal penalty for seducing a single girl, regardless of whether or not she has become pregnant, is a *ndovu* (40 strings of discs plus a number of dog's and porpoise teeth). The youth has no valuables of his own and relies upon his father and uncles to pay. The amount goes to the girl's relatives on both sides. She may be beaten, but a fine is never imposed upon her; on the other hand, her bride price is reduced. Usually the interested parties try to force the pair into marriage. The kinsfolk of the youth thus avoid a double payment, that of a seduction penalty as well as the bride price. In addition the kinfolk of the girl are saved from having to face the shame of a public admission of her misbehavior.

If pregnancy has occurred a marriage has the further advantage of solving the illegitimacy problem, for the people soon forget that the child was born too soon. If the marriage offer is refused, the relationship between the father and his offspring passes unrecognized. He does not contribute toward its support, and he can make no demands upon it. As a rule, one of the girl's brothers takes the child, but it may stay with her and ultimately become absorbed into the household of her husband, in which case his relatives behave as though he were, in fact, the begetter.

Matters are more complicated when seducer and paramour belong to the same clan. People say that the offense is then truly shocking and that in the past the guilty couple would have been put to death. But they could not quote a single instance of such a killing, and I suspect them of exaggerating. Early in my stay they used to add that since the Government banned violence, they were obliged to resort to such substitute punishments as turning the pair out of the village. A fine was ruled out, they stated, by the overlapping of the boy's and the girl's kindreds; and, even if this situation did not apply in individual cases, the boy's relatives would be too angry with him to offer anything and the girl's too appalled at her conduct to accept. To take valuables for an outrage of this order would imply that any evil could be compounded.

As I came to know the place better I found that this second statement was equally at variance with the facts. No matter how serious the misconduct, offenders are never pushed out of the settlement to live in the forest; moreover, in every case of a technical seduction (to copulate with a girl from a distant community is in no sense classed as wrong), the boy's and the girl's kindreds do overlap. When, during my stay, a young man was found to have committed clan incest with a girl to whom, admittedly, he was genealogically only distantly connected, her relatives demanded payment and his obliged. The villagers not directly implicated said to one another that they were utterly disgusted; yet they refrained from making open reproaches in the presence of the couple or their close kin. The youth must have felt embarrassed, nevertheless, for within a fortnight he had gone away to seek employment on a plantation.

This episode led to my hearing of a similar incident that had taken place a year earlier at Paupau. The pair had been married off to each other forthwith and seemed to be suffering no social discrimination. (It is also unlikely that their future misfortunes, if any, will be attributed to divine judgment, as might happen in certain parts of Melanesia: I shall explain later that the Guadalcanal religious system is lacking in moral content.)

Preliminaries to Marriage

The members of the parent generation insist on selecting the partners in all marriages. They give several reasons. First, everything relating to bride price is necessarily their concern. They own all the valuables and have to collect and distribute them. Moreover, it is felt that young people would be swayed too much by physical attraction, whereas a senior keeps character foremost in his mind. Beauty fades, but a partnership founded on industry, good temper, and ability to cooperate with others may be expected to endure for a lifetime. The kinsfolk of the spouse are a further consideration. Because brothers-in-law are potential helpers, a girl from a large family is likely to be much sought after. Similarly, a boy with a village leader as a near kinsman is more acceptable than one whose immediate relatives are nonentities. Many men also think that at least one son should be wedded to a girl of their clan, thereby ensuring grandchildren for the replenishment of the group. In the past, before the prohibition on fighting, it was also often a deliberate policy to widen the circle of kinsmen by arranging for dependents to marry into other settlements.

Nowadays betrothal is almost unknown, but once upon a time headmen made a practice of affiancing their young sons, and occasionally their young uterine nephews, to the infant daughter or infant uterine niece of an important householder living in some other community. These marriages resembled the dynastic unions of the Hapsburgs, the Bourbons, and the Medici in that they aimed at confirming traditional alliances or at creating new ties. The contract was sealed by the presentation of a *ndovu* to the girl's father and maternal uncles, who kept the wealth intact for the time being lest the plan should fall through for one reason or another and the discs and teeth have to be returned.

At present, the first moves always come from the young man's side but they are delayed until he is about twenty-two or twenty-three years of age. The obligation to find the bride rests primarily on the father (if the father is dead, then on his oldest brother), though discussion with the uncles on both sides is usual. In the event of disagreement, the father has the final say, but generally he picks a girl whom he feels sure everybody will consider suitable. He then asks someone related to both himself and her kin to press his claims. The fact that there is a go-between means that a refusal need not result in the breaking-off of social relations. The girl's father's views are the deciding factor, but he also refers the question to his brothers, brothers-in-law, and eldest son, who, when the father grows old, will replace him as her protector. Once consent is assured the plan is put to the young people for their approval. It is agreed that a forced marriage would be undesirable, and if either the boy or the girl is unwilling, negotiations are stopped. The boy's father then tries someone else.

A couple determined to marry against the wishes of their kindred are forced to elope. The youth, to demonstrate his honorable intentions, invites someone distantly related to them both to run away with them, and all three take refuge with still another kinsman in a neighboring settlement. Here they remain till the opposition has subsided. The girl's relatives are too afraid for her reputation to challenge her tenacity, and sooner or later her father and uncles surrender.

Girls' Puberty Rites

We are now ready to deal with the rites associated with a girl's coming of age. It was best to postpone the discussion till this point because the various payments have a bearing on the bride price handed over during the wedding.

Boys may once have had to pass through an initiation ceremony, but if so, all memory of it has been lost. Girls, however, still submit to the ordeal of face-marking, which is in some respects comparable to male puberty rites. The proper time is described as "when the breasts begin to swell" (not, it should be noted, at the first menstruation). But the operation is expensive, and if the relatives have had recent calls on their resources some delay may be necessary. Probably the normal age is around fifteen.

The father makes the decision after consultation with his own and his wife's brothers. These men not only have an interest in his daughter but also provide a part of the fee, though, like him, they depend upon contributions from other relatives. The first job is to engage an expert in face-marking, someone who has learned the appropriate skills and the accompanying magic from either his father or a maternal uncle. It is felt that this man ought to belong to a different clan from the girl's; were he to be from the same clan she might be stricken blind by the operation. The expert fixes the date and then asks the younger people of the village to assemble the night before at the girl's parents' house.

The youths, the maidens, the newly-married husbands, and the newly-married wives gather round the dwelling after dusk and spend the hours of darkness singing. The females sit in a circle with the girl to be marked in the center and chant songs called *loloele;* at intervals the males take over with ballads for soloists and chorus (*silaru*). The aim is to keep her awake so that her dulled senses will prevent her from feeling too much pain the next day. From time to time her mother and closer women relatives and affines offer food to the guests; her father, uncles, and closer men relatives supply them with tobacco and betel nut.

The operator has a good night's rest and arrives on the scene soon after dawn. The father presents him with at least 10 strings of discs and 20 dog's teeth, and the operator then calls up his assistants, from half a dozen to ten young men, none of them a near kinsman of the girl. The assistants take her to the shelter that her father and uncles have erected in the bush some time previously and proceed to hold her still while the expert does his work. The father and uncles keep well out of earshot lest they should hear her screams and become upset.

The designs are etched on the face with the pointed bone of a flying fox. (Tattooing would not show on the dark brown skin, and inks are not used.) There may be concentric circles marked out by drawing guide lines with charcoal around several pieces of bamboo of different diameters; there may be arcs of larger circles, herringbone patterns, designs of squares or diamonds, zigzags, or a patchwork of lines. Each series has a different name.

When one side of the face is completed the operator pauses and sends off an assistant to the girl's senior maternal uncle to say how very weary he is— so tired, indeed, that he wishes to stop. The lad returns with a basket of valuables approximately equivalent to the amount already paid by the father. The man now starts work on the other side of the face. He ends up by piercing the girl's nasal septum to enable her to wear a nose stick of shell or walrus ivory.

The whole process takes upwards of six hours, depending on the operator's patience and the girl's fortitude.

Word is now sent to the women of the hamlet. They arrive with another payment for the operator, which consists of as many valuables as the father and the uncle have given together, perhaps 20 strings of discs and 20 dog's teeth, collected from the members of the two subclans. He therefore receives about one *ndovu* as a reward for his efforts. The women also bring a small gift of dog's and porpoise teeth for each of the assistants, as well as several bowls of food, including pork and fish. The boys then depart and the women carry the girl back to the village. She spends two days in bed, and they then lead her to the beach for a bath. While she is in the water they rub the scabs off her face. This is repeated two days later.

A few boys have marks cut on their face, but they never complete the set. They act on their own initiative and generally seek out an apprentice operator who is glad to practice on them and does not demand a fee.

The Bridal Payment

After the prospective bride has been selected, the next step is the collection of the wealth that must be handed over for her. The boy's father makes the initial move, though, directly and indirectly, he is responsible for only half the amount. He approaches his eldest brother-in-law (the potential groom's senior maternal uncle), who has to find the other half, and they decide together how much to offer. Their prestige is enhanced by giving a large sum, and they do not attempt to lower each other's bids. The usual price for a girl of spotless reputation when she is from the same village is 3 or 4 *ndovu* (120 to 160 strings of discs, 120 to 160 dog's teeth, and 300 to 400 porpoise teeth), but if she lives in a different settlement, and will therefore be cut off from regular daily contact with her near kin, an extra *ndovu* is needed as special compensation to them. A headman may give a bigger payment for a wife for his sons, and he also hopes to obtain more when his daughters marry.

The father now goes around to the householders of his subclan and perhaps to a few of his other close relatives. Some of them may have more immediate obligations to fulfill, but the majority promise a contribution, if only a string or two or a couple of dozen teeth. Simultaneously, the maternal uncle calls on the members of his subclan and close relatives for similar contributions.

As soon as the preliminaries are completed and help assured, the boy's father and maternal uncle fix the day for the gathering of the valuables in the father's house. The youth sets off early in the morning on a visit, for under no circumstances is he allowed to witness the proceedings. In the past, lack of property would have precluded the groom's providing any of the bride price, but today, while employed, the more enterprising of the natives try to turn part of their wages into strings of discs—at 70 cents (5 shillings) for each fathom length—which they hand to the father.

Every man who has made a donation attends the gathering of the bride price in person. He is accompanied by somebody else, preferably an outsider, who, in the event of later argument, can testify that he did in fact do his duty by his young kinsman. Generally, the total accumulated is substantial but not quite enough. At this stage the village headman may help out, though most of what is still needed comes from distant relatives of the bridegroom, individuals of about thirty years of age who are beginning to establish themselves as house-holders of substance. They declare these gifts to be "alive" (*mauri*) and expect them to be carefully remembered; such valuables become "dead" (*mae*) only when at a future wedding, after the delay of a decade or longer, the groom himself discharges the debt by making the exact equivalent available. Although the givers receive no interest and thus can scarcely be said to have made a profitable investment, they still reap some benefit. They place the recipient under an obligation, and hence ensure his future cooperation; in addition, they overcome the theft risk, always a consideration in a community that is without banks.

At one wedding I attended the bridegroom's father provided 20 strings and 20 dog's teeth of his own; the paternal grandfather 12 strings and 100 porpoise teeth; the two paternal uncles together 15 strings, 40 dog's teeth, and 60 porpoise teeth; eight other patrilateral kinsmen together 27 strings, 20 dog's teeth, and 10 porpoise teeth; the eldest maternal uncle 20 strings and 20 dog's teeth of his own; the two other maternal uncles together 25 strings, 40 dog's teeth, and 20 porpoise teeth; ten other matrilateral kinsmen together 30 strings, 20 dog's teeth, and 100 porpoise teeth; and five very distant relatives together 11 "live" strings and 25 "live" porpoise teeth. All told, twenty-eight individuals took part in the transaction.

Next, the boy's father sends a message to the father of the girl saying when he proposes to deliver the bride price. Neither he nor his son attends, but everyone else who has contributed goes along. A man selected by the father carries the valuables in a basket on his shoulder and, on arrival, deposits the basket before the door of the girl's father's house. Her mother quickly takes it inside for examination later.

The girl does not appear, but the members of her father's and her maternal uncles' subclans, as well as some other kinsmen, are assembled to make the guests welcome and offer them tobacco and betel nut. Hosts and guests talk together for an hour or so, and then the women produce sufficient vegetable foods for the visitors to make a good meal. The girl's father presents the dishes to the boy's father's representative, who divides them into two, half for the boy's patrilateral kin and half for his matrilateral kin. The representative himself distributes the first lot, the senior maternal uncle the second. The party may eat a little then and there, but they carry the bulk home.

Next day the girl's father and senior maternal uncle deal with the bride price. Naturally they are pleased if it is large, but they raise no difficulties should the amount be less than they had expected. Their only reaction is to make degrogatory remarks to the neighbors, and soon the gossip spreads far and wide.

The bride price is split into two approximately equal portions, one for the girl's patrilateral relatives and the other for her matrilateral relatives; it is apportioned by her father and her senior maternal uncle, respectively. The payment previously described was divided as follows. First the 160 strings, 160 dog's teeth, and 315 porpoise teeth were separated into the two piles—80 strings, 80 dog's teeth, and 140 porpoise teeth for the patrilateral kin, and 80 strings, 80 dog's teeth, and 175 porpoise teeth for the matrilateral kin. The father then took 25 strings, 20 dog's teeth, and 40 porpoise teeth; of these he gave away 5 strings and the porpoise teeth to wipe out three "live" debts. Next he offered 15 strings and 20 dog's teeth to his only brother and 10 strings and 20 dog's teeth to the leading man of his subclan. The remainder of this heap went in approximately equal amounts to the four other householders of the subclan and two men from outside. The maternal uncle kept 21 strings and 60 dog's teeth and gave his three brothers each 12 strings and 20 dog's teeth. To the other householder from the subclan, a youngish man, he offered 8 strings and 15 dog's teeth. What was left (15 strings, 5 dog's teeth, and 115 porpoise teeth) went in varying sums to five kinsmen of different clans. In all, there were twenty recipients.

Within a few weeks the bride's kinsfolk begin preparations for a counterpresentation of foodstuffs, for which, however, the bridegroom's kinsfolk are required to pay. Each man who received 10 strings or more of the bride price provides at least one pig, and the rest furnish cooked vegetables, in amounts roughly proportional to their share of the valuables. Ordinarily, there are from six to eight carcasses, from twelve to twenty bowls of yams mashed with coconut cream, and many baskets and packages of other delicacies.

The bride's father gives three or four days' notice of when the party will arrive with the gifts, but as the time approaches, he and the senior maternal uncle nominate a kinsman as their representative so that they can stay at home. The greater part of the morning is spent in catching the pigs and making the puddings, and the visitors do not reach the bridegroom's father's house till the early afternoon. The beasts, still alive, are bound to a pole for easy carrying and are ornamented with flowers and festoons of brightly-colored leaves and fruit. The people set them up in a long row with the bowls and baskets of vegetables arranged in front. A few persons, women as well as men, then come forward and leave nearby such personal belongings as spears, bowls, or baskets. These folk are the peripheral kinsmen of the bride who have helped with the display. They feel that their labors entitle them to some slight recompense.

The bridegroom's kin spend an hour or two admiring the show. The principal contributors to the bride price, including the father and senior maternal uncle, then step forward carrying sets of strings of discs. Each selects a pig and lays his strings across its back. The amount should be almost, but not quite, the animal's value on the open market. If, as sometimes happens, one or more of the pigs is not covered, a distant relative may come to the rescue. His payment is then a "living" debt and must be redeemed on some similar occasion in the future. (Once such debts had to be memorized; today, a creditor who has received sufficient education keeps a written record.) The boy's father, and, to some extent, his uncles, are ashamed if any of the beasts remain unbought and have to be taken home again.

The lesser contributors then seize the personal belongings one by one. "Whose is this?" they ask in turn. The owner calls out his name and receives a few teeth. Not until everything has been disposed of do the donors of the pigs collect their payments.

The groom's father and maternal uncle first make sure that each of the bride's senior kinsmen receives a portion of the food for the return journey— avoiding giving anyone articles that he himself presented—and then distribute the supplies in the normal way. The pigs can now be killed and the puddings taken away.

All is now ready for the girl to leave home. On a day agreed upon some of the young people, drawn mainly from the groom's father's and mother's sub-clans, go across to fetch the bride. They bring her to the groom's mother's dwelling, where she remains for several weeks, ostensibly to be taught house-keeping. At length, the groom's father arranges for a residence to be built for the couple, always near his own so that for the time being he and his wife can keep an eye on things. The furnishings and cooking utensils are supplied by the girl's parents.

The natives offer two explanations for the bride-price custom. They say that the girl's relatives are justified in demanding reimbursement both for their expenditure on her face-marking and also for their loss of her services. Although the subclan retains its numerical strength through the marriage of its female members, these women transfer their labors to the husband and his kinsfolk. A married sister continues seeing her brothers, especially if she lives in the same village, but performs only occasional duties for them. For serious help they must wait till her sons reach maturity.

Two further points that could be stressed receive no comment. The pay-ments are an important factor in ensuring that the groom will treat his wife well and that she will not leave him for trivial reasons. Women are prepared to accept a heavy blow from time to time without making much fuss, but if a husband injures his spouse severely she leaves him. Should she refuse to go back, as she is entitled to do, her relatives retain the bride price. The man's kin, having already beggared themselves, are unwilling to make a second effort on his behalf, and he is therefore denied a substitute partner. Young husbands realize the severity of the penalty, and the majority of them take care to conduct them-selves with propriety.

About five years before my visit a young man named Hali accused his newly married wife of infidelity. The charge was without foundation, and when he persisted she swore at him. (She told him to eat his mother's excrement.) Enraged, he took his knife and stabbed her about the shoulders and thigh. Her life was not in danger, but her brothers took her away. Later her father and senior maternal uncle gave his father and senior maternal uncle a set of 4 strings each "for shame's sake," but none of the other valuables was returned. News of the incident came to the ears of the district officer, and he promptly brought Hali to trial and sentenced him to a term of imprisonment. He was freed long before my arrival, and I found him a hot-tempered but likeable companion. His relatives, however, steadfastly declined to take any interest in arranging for his remarriage; moreover, the girls whom he fancied without exception rejected his advances.

Divorce

Divorce is rare even before the birth of children and very rare indeed afterwards. Apart from cruelty, the grounds are incompatibility and adultery, and people discussing the question in the abstract, with no specific instance in mind, always insist that the wife has as much right as the husband to break up the union. Yet, in an overwhelming majority of cases, it is the man who takes the initiative. The reason is obvious. Only when he has been guilty of causing bodily harm to his spouse are her relatives permitted to retain the bride price. If the separation is the result of the inability of the couple to pull together or the unfaithfulness of one partner, then at least some portion of the valuables must be handed over. The amount depends on the length of time that the marriage has endured. If the wedding took place a few months before, the rule is that everything has to be returned; but a token sum suffices if the pair already have a young family—perhaps half a dozen strings each from the father and the senior maternal uncle. Inevitably, the men who received the payments are unwilling to give anything back, and should the woman become restive about her husband's behavior, they exert pressure upon her to overlook his faults. It follows that divorce occurs almost exclusively when the man cannot tolerate the woman or when she has been unfaithful. She tends to suppress her dislikes and to put up with his extramarital affairs.

It is to be noted that a woman's sterility is not acceptable as a reason for divorcing her, and also that her relatives are not expected to supply another mate under such circumstances. On the other hand, a wife who dies soon after the marriage must either be replaced—though never by her true sister—or else the bride price is recoverable. Even if her death does not happen for years, after the birth of children, a small part of the payment is offered, usually a few strings supplied by the father and the senior maternal uncle or, if they are no longer alive, by her brothers.

A match between a widow and the deceased husband's brother is also forbidden. When a man dies the widow's relatives return up to a maximum of half the bride price, the precise quantity again depending on the duration of the union, so that she will be free to join her brothers. Should she now contract a second marriage the payment goes to her own relatives, not to those of her former husband. Half the normal sum may be offered for a young childless widow, rather less for one who has a family.

Behavior of Affines

A man and his wife's parents, uncles, and aunts—and a woman and her husband's parents, uncles, and aunts—have to treat one another with mutual respect. They use personal names in address, but displays of anger are absolutely forbidden, as are impolite expressions and references to sex or excreta. The parents-in-law are thus prevented from chiding a husband or wife who has failed to perform the ordinary household duties. Requests for help are permitted, and gifts of food are constantly exchanged.

Even greater reserve is enjoined between a man and his sisters-in-law (the sisters of his wife and the wives of his brothers) and between a woman and her brothers-in-law (the brothers of her husband and the husbands of her sisters). Personal names are again allowed, but, in addition to avoiding violence and loose talk, they have to beware of taking anything directly from one another's hands. If a woman wishes to offer her brother-in-law a meal she sets the dish on the floor in front of him. Further, it is said that they ought not to sleep under the same roof, though in practice the conventions are satisfied if a screen of mats is set up between them. There is no difficulty when a man accompanies his wife on a visit to her sister: he and the sister's husband move over to the men's club for the night. A problem arises mainly on the rare occasion when two brothers and their families find it necessary to stay in a hut alongside their gardens, perhaps because a pig has been destroying the fences. The taboo seems to be associated with notions of the desirability of preserving subclan unity. It is argued that a regulation hindering a man from enjoying free intercourse with his brothers' wives and his wife's sisters removes sexual temptation and so contributes to the harmony of the group.

The relations of brothers-in-law are characterized by easy amity, and an oft-repeated saying has it that they are almost as close as brothers but engage in fewer arguments. The reason is to be sought in the rules of matrilineal inheritance. The children of a man's sisters' husbands are his heirs, and his children, in turn, become the heirs of his wife's brothers. A woman is always able to appeal to her brothers in a dispute with her husband, but she cannot rely implicitly on the brothers' ultimate sympathy. They listen to her story and offer to act as mediators; they may even be obliged to rebuke the husband, but their final counsel is likely to be reconciliation rather than separation. Divorce would mean not only surrender of their share of the bride price, as was mentioned, but also loss of valued assistance.

Sisters-in-law have a similar understanding, except that their common interests are not so overwhelmingly important. Yet the wives of brothers live in the same hamlet and are thus in daily contact, and sisters often pay visits to their brothers' households, calls that are just as constantly returned.

The term for husband or wife is *mburanga-na;* for son-in-law or daughter-in-law, parents-in-law, and the brothers and sisters of the parents-in-law, *vungau-na;* for brothers-in-law, if a man is speaking, and sisters-in-law if a woman is speaking, *uta;* for sisters-in-law if a man is speaking, and brothers-in-law if a woman is speaking, *iva-na.*

3

Rearing a Family

ALL PARENTS WANT CHILDREN, the father as much as the mother, even though his offspring do not belong to his clan. For the first couple of months, nevertheless, the baby remains exclusively in the mother's care. She holds it in a sling of bark cloth on her hip, fondles it gently, offers it her breast as soon as it begins to cry, and at night sleeps with it nestled alongside her. She is alive to the need for cleanliness and bathes it daily in a bowl of warm water, nowadays, if possible, with soap. Should it soil her she wipes it tenderly with a few soft leaves or an old piece of rag before rubbing herself down. Soon she recognizes the signs that it is about to relieve itself, and then she tries to lift it away from her body. She does not attempt bladder and bowel training till after it is toddling, perhaps early in the second year, when she may scold it or administer a light tap if it makes a mess. By this time she follows the practice of carrying it outside first thing in the morning and after it has sucked its fill, pushes it out at arm's length, and encourages it with grunting noises. Most children of about three have learned to control the sphincter muscles and err only occasionally in being careless in removing the traces of excrement. (Pebbles, twigs, or leaves serve this purpose.) The father, in particular, is cross if a youngster who is backward shames him in the presence of others, but as a rule he does no more than growl and express the hope that the child will soon conduct itself with more propriety.

Fathers are not allowed to hold the infant for more than a few minutes until after the third month. Before that it is said to be too fragile to be submitted to their clumsiness. They then lift it up eagerly on returning home in the evenings, place it astride the hip, rock it from side to side, and croon to it while the wife cooks the evening meal.

Mushy foods, at first premasticated yams and bananas, are given at about the sixth or seventh month. The mother or father sits with the baby on the knees and pushes the pap into its mouth with a finger. Later the soft flesh

31

of immature coconuts is added, as are steamed and crushed green vegetables. By about eighteen months mashed yam is considered suitable, and shortly afterwards other items of the diet are gradually brought in. Fish and pork, which are supposed to be indigestible, are not allowed till about the fourth year.

Weaning is generally a gentle process. At the end of the second year or early in the third, the mother begins withholding her breast, unless the child is ill or miserable; perhaps she may also make mild fun of it for behaving like a newly-born infant should it ask to be suckled. Sudden effort in weaning is necessary only if the woman becomes pregnant too soon. Then she at once smears her nipples with tobacco juice and bitter herbs. I have known women to burst into tears at the sight of a child's bewilderment as it rolled its tongue around its mouth with distaste after attempting to suck.

Moving About

Walking is regarded as a natural accomplishment that will be mastered in time, and parents and relatives do not urge the child to begin until it shows some inclination of its own to do so. Once it can stand up, they offer a finger or hold out a stick to give support as it totters about. Bystanders, too, may beckon it across to them and run forward should it appear to be in danger of falling. Swimming seems to come just as easily. At first the father and mother take it to the shallow brooks that abound in the area and show it how to splash about and become accustomed to the feel of running water. Later, soon after the end of the second year, they play with it at the edge of the creeks flowing through the village. They do not give instructions concerning the motions of the legs and arms, but soon—always before the third year—every child can not only keep afloat but paddle forward without touching the bottom. Later still, when it starts mixing with other youngsters, it imitates them and is soon diving and swimming below the surface. I have never heard of a child's drowning—except, perhaps, on the rare occasions when a canoe has foundered in midocean in a storm and caused the loss of the crew and passengers.

The parents are ready with comfort if the child falls down, is burned by fire, or hurts itself in some other way; but after massaging the bruises, binding up the cuts, and making certain that no serious damage has been done, they pet it only if they do not happen to be busy at the moment. They would not think of neglecting the cooking or gardening in order to sit for hours with a little girl or boy who was suffering from some minor injury. "There, there, there, the pain will soon finish," they murmur. "Stay still for a little on the mat here close by me while I go on with what I'm doing." I also noted that people never attribute personality, much less malice, to inanimate objects; they do not sooth a child by telling it that a stick had set out to trip it up or water become hot for the express purpose of causing a scald. "You must keep your eyes open," they say, or, "You ought to take care how you go."

Moral Training

Two virtues, generosity and respect for property, are inculcated from the eighteenth month onward—that is to say, from the age when the child can walk about and eat bananas and other things regarded as delicacies. At this stage no explanations are given, and the parents merely insist that food must be shared with any playmate who happens to be present and that goods belonging to other villagers must be left undisturbed. A toddler presented with a piece of fruit is told to give half to "So-and-so," and should the order be resisted, the adult ignores all protests and breaks a piece off to hand to the child's companion. Similarly, although sometimes callers are cautioned to put their baskets on a shelf out of reach, any meddling brings forth the rebuke, "That belongs to your uncle. Put it down." Disobedience is followed by snatching away the item in question from the child and returning it to the owner.

In time, when the child has passed into its fourth or fifth year, it is acknowledged to have at last attained the understanding to be able to take in what the adults say. Therefore, adults now accompany demands with reasoned instruction. One day when I was paying a call on a neighbor, Mwane-Anuta, I heard him warn his second son Mbule, who probably had not yet reached the age of five, to stop being so greedy. "I saw your mother give you those nuts," Mwane-Anuta reiterated. "Don't pretend she didn't. Running behind the house so that Penggoa wouldn't know! That is bad, very bad. Now then, show me, how many? Five left. Very well, offer three to Penggoa immediately." He then went on to tell me how important it was for children to learn to think of others so that in later life they would win the respect of their fellows.

On another occasion during a meal I found Mwane-Anuta and his wife teaching their three sons how to eat properly. "Now Mbule," said his mother, "you face the rest of us so that we can all see you aren't taking too much. And you, Konana, run outside and ask Misika from next door to join you. His mother's not home yet, and I expect he's hungry. Your belly's not the only one, my boy." "Yes," Mwane-Anuta added. "Give a thought to those you run about with, and they'll give a thought to you." At that point the mother called over the eldest lad, Kure, and placed the basket of yams for me in his hands. "There, you carry that over to our guest and say that it is good to have him with us this evening," she whispered to him. The gesture was characteristic. I noted that always when meals were served to visitors the children acted as waiters. Why was this, I wanted to know. "Teaching, teaching," Mwane-Anuta replied. "This is how we train our young to behave."

With the passage of the years promptings become unnecessary, and older boys and girls divide their food as a matter of course, unless they happen to be very hungry or have received something that is normally not available, such as biscuits and candy from a visiting anthropologist.

Once understanding has been achieved, the adults also deliver homilies about touching other people's belongings. They explained to me that drilling in the rules of ownership was vital because, unlike Europeans, they were without locks and keys and so could not protect their houses and goods. "White men need only say to their children once or twice, 'Don't touch what isn't yours'—that is enough because you can all shut up your boxes. Not so with us! We have to go on talking until we're sure that our youngsters won't even think of picking up tools or clothing from the neighbors' dwellings." A parent on a visit with a five- or six-year-old keeps up a constant stream of reminders. "No, that belongs to So-and-so—replace it at once"; "Put that down this instant: if you were to break it what would happen?—you'd have a hiding, that's what"; "Stop, stop—think of where you are—this isn't our house." A child who comes home with something new is always subjected to interrogation. He has to say where the object came from and who gave it to him. If his answers are unsatisfactory the father takes it away and tries to find the owner.

I should add that during my stay in Longgu, despite calls at all hours from children and adults, nothing I brought with me was stolen—a contrast to what has happened in some of the other communities in which I have worked.

Punishment

Neither parent is averse to administering a light slap on the buttocks or a cuff on the shoulders once weaning has taken place, but until the child enters its fourth year there is a noticeable preference for encouraging good behavior by threats. The elders begin by telling tales of the giants called *umou* that are supposed to inhabit the remote mountains. These beings, they say, are ready to pounce on naughty boys and girls and carry them off to a cave, where the bodies are cooked and eaten. "A giant is listening behind that tree there," the father or mother exclaims. "He's come because he knows you've been disobedient. If you don't do what I ask I'll invite him over here to take you away. Already I can hear him crunching your bones as he eats you up." Some reference may also be made to any stranger who has recently passed through the village. "You saw that dark-skinned man going by yesterday evening?" Mwane-Anuta reminded Mbule. "Well, where he lives they buy little boys. The big basket he had over his shoulder is for popping them in. If you don't stop your games for a bit and fetch my pipe from the house, as I've told you to do twice now, I'll offer you to him when he returns."

At other times I have heard fathers warn a youngster that unless it mends its ways they will inform the maternal uncle and request his intervention. Such conduct may be disapproved by those not directly concerned. This happened to Ohaoha, a young married man with a son aged four or five. He had lost his patience when the boy persisted in throwing stones at a valuable pair of hunting dogs, rapped him on the back with a stick, and exclaimed, "When your mother's brother Sasaka gets home I'm going to relate to him a full account of your doings. I'm sure that once he's heard he'll give you such a hiding you won't be able to sit down for the pain. Don't come then to your mother or to me for sympathy! We'll be pleased to see you cry." At this point Ohaoha's own uncle, who lived next door, interposed and criticized him for making the lad afraid of his fellow clansmen. "You're a fool setting up barriers like that; sisters' sons oughtn't to shiver at the name of their mother's brothers."

Still another threat, usually held in reserve till the child is a little older, is that if he continually misbehaves he will be sure to arouse the anger of somebody who has a knowledge of sorcery. Each hamlet seems to have a stock victim as an awful example, and he is invariably said to have been a contemporary of the speaker's father. In the hamlet where my house was situated it was the boy Kole; he became the object of black magic after he had stolen, thrown stones at animals, refused to run errands, remained with his mother when he ought to have been out fishing with his father, fought with his sisters, and altogether made a nuisance of himself.

Perhaps the best technique of all for securing conformity is the pretense of withdrawing affection. This can be most effective, but not every parent is capable of acting for a period as if the child did not exist. Those who are may refuse to take any notice for upwards of a couple of hours. The youngster is at first angry at being brushed aside and having its remarks ignored. Then it starts to cry, but when it has learned that even tears will not be heeded it either sits in abject despair or tries to help with the adults' tasks. Eventually the father or the mother relents, and there is a great reconciliation.

Never, at any time, is a child told that it will not be given any dinner. The threat would be useless, for it could always run off to an uncle or an aunt.

Severe punishment is the last resort. Beatings are uncommon but may be administered by the mother as well as the father. Indeed, on no less than three occasions I watched a man restrain his wife from hitting their offspring too severely. "Enough, enough," said one of them. "You'll break the boy's skin. He has suffered, and you've taught him his lesson. He'll listen to you from now on."

Paternal and maternal uncles, and aunts also, have the right to whip an unruly nephew or niece but seldom do so. They hesitate to arouse the parents' resentment, even though etiquette would forbid any expression of ill feeling.

It should be mentioned that older children, from the age of, say, six, may be struck not only for downright misconduct but also for extreme carelessness. Thus, Ngangenda belabored his seven-year-old son with a stick around the shoulders when the boy wrestled with a companion too vigorously and thereby set an old wound on his leg bleeding again. It is true that Ngangenda was cross because his advice had been ignored, but he assured me that the beating was more a penalty for folly. Kapini suffered similarly, this time at the hands of his mother, when, jumping about on a high platform, he slipped and fell on a sharp stone. A neighbor reproved Niaseka, however, for slapping his son for upsetting a bowl of nearly-boiling water over himself. "But the lad is in pain—he's scalded his leg. Don't be so cruel," cried the woman from the house across the road when she heard the commotion.

Once I also saw a man pick up his daughter, who was about six years old, and drop her from a height of 3 feet into a pool of water. On several occasions different people either tied a lad's hands behind his back or fastened him with a rope around the waist to a post. Saa had become enraged when his son first lost a tin containing a valuable necklace and then broke a bottle of magical toothache medicine. He bound the boy's wrists together, gave his cheeks a resounding thwack, and drove him off into the bush, whence an aunt rescued him at the end of half an hour.

Learning about Kinship

As the mother suckles her infant she says to it, *"Nggie, nggie,* I am your *nggie,"* and ordinarily this is the first word the child utters. My friends explained that it is the substitute for the normal expression for mother, *tike,* which is too difficult for a baby's tiny tongue and lips. We can therefore translate it as "mummie" or "mum." The father similarly uses "daddie" or "dad" (*ngga*) instead of *mama.* To begin with the child applies *nggie* to everybody, but after a short period this comes to be reserved for females, and the males are all *ngga.* The women who act as nurses are, in fact, mostly classified with the mother, and they make wheedling noises and remark, "Good, good; you know now what to call me. I also am your mummie. Here, child, suck my breast." (A woman who has no milk offers suitable food instead.) In the same way, many of the men who live nearby regard themselves as equivalent to the father and are pleased to be included as *ngga.* This is even true of the mother's brothers, who do not as yet insist on being called by a distinguishing title.

The proper kinship terms are adopted gradually, and nobody seems to mind if a child of five or six miscalls his mother's brothers "father" (*mama*) and his father's brothers "maternal uncle" (*sa'i*). The elders do not rush in with corrections but instead shake their heads tolerantly. "This is unimportant," they laughed to me. "He'll learn which relative is which in time. And, anyway, maternal and paternal uncles are similar to one another. They're both a sort of father." Not until another year has passed does an average child know exactly what the difference is. He then points, on the one hand, to his father's brothers and the men in the same category, indicating that they are "fathers"; and, on the other hand, to his mother's brothers. The latter and he, he insists sententiously, are fellow clansmen. (But if asked what clanship implies he is as yet unable to give an answer: information about the rules of land tenure comes later, around the age of puberty.)

Children of this age—from seven on—move about the village freely from hamlet to hamlet, visiting their different close kinsmen. Although still unaware of the details of the relationships and the exact genealogical links, they are conscious of the status of their hosts: that this one is a maternal uncle, that one an older brother, another a father's sister, and so on.

Adults, discussing the situation, maintain that food lies behind the youngsters' knowledge. "When I was a little boy my father's brothers used to take me to their houses, give me something to eat, and say that they were the same as my real father," Mwane-Anuta told me. "And my mother's brothers took me also, put yams in my hand, and explained that they and I were *sa'i*. If I was hungry, they used to go on, I was to ask them for a meal. What happened? I knew they'd always be kind and feed me—so that's how I came to understand about the ties of kin."

A person may donate food to any relative—indeed, is expected to do so. But direct requests are made only to near relatives. It is considered shameful, no matter what the circumstances, to approach distant kinsmen. Etiquette also enforces the acceptance of all gifts. If someone who has just finished a heavy supper is invited by a neighbor to partake of a further basket of vegetables, he is bound to say "yes." He nibbles away for a while before excusing himself and going home.

At a slightly later stage, when a child is big enough to take responsibility, the elders reinforce their various demands with a reference to all the earlier feeding. "When you were hungry we took care to stuff your belly," say the uncles and aunts. "You must think of what we did for you and repay our efforts by doing things for us. You took yams then: now you can even things up by helping in our work."

Children's Games

Guadalcanal villages are by ordinary Melanesian standards fairly large, and although there are not enough boys and girls to form regular gangs, each child is able to find a handful of companions of approximately his own age from the surrounding hamlets. The most popular game with children between the ages of six and twelve is hide-and-seek, known as *tautauporo*. The group selects one youngster and tells him to close his eyes; the rest then run away and conceal themselves. After about a minute he sets off on his search, and as he catches sight of someone he calls out the name. Should anybody remain undiscovered after five minutes all gather round to decide whether the undiscovered child had played unfairly—by going further than a reasonable distance or perhaps by relying too much on the help of a grownup. The child then closes his eyes again, and the proceedings are repeated. (It is thought that he would go bald if he was "out" only once.) Another then takes his place, and so the play continues till boredom sets in. Other pastimes include a form of hopscotch, ninepins with shells standing upright and a small coconut for bowling, rather aimless throwing of oranges or other fruit, and, recently, cricket and football. Then there are also water sports, such as races with toy canoes or rafts and fights between teams pretending to be sharks and crocodiles.

Children also play at housekeeping. Sometimes they take along their juniors, who, however, do not remain interested for long. They put up a framework of saplings and tie on coconut-leaf mats, which they plait themselves in a rough-and-ready sort of way. Occasionally they beg some raw food and prepare it; or they catch birds, bats, and rats with bows and arrows. Many times, too,

I have seen them hold weddings, including all the formality of the handing-over of bride price. Various items serve instead of the valuables that the grownups use—tiny pebbles instead of dog's and porpoise teeth, the long flowers of a nut tree for strings of shell discs, and rats or lizards for pigs.[1]

When first the youngsters pretend to keep house they make no sexual distinction in the allocation of the tasks. Boys and girls together erect the shelters, plait the mats, cook the food, and fetch the water. But within a year or so, although they continue to play in company, the members of each group restrict themselves to the work appropriate to their sex. The boys leave the cooking and water carrying to the girls, who, in turn, refuse to help with the building.

Later still, when the boys are about thirteen or a little older, they want to be by themselves. If they come across a girl, they torment her by calling her names, pushing her, or throwing stones. (They cannot pull her hair because it is cut short.)

During this play period, when the children are in small bands of five or six, the elders hate to see them fighting. At the slightest sign of trouble some bystander calls out at the top of his voice that the pair are brothers or cousins (or sisters or brother and sister) and that it is therefore wrong of them to so much as think of striking one another. "Say what you like to him," said one man to his son. "Call him a fool—tell him he's stupid if you want to. But never never punch your brother or your cousin. That would be an evil thing to do." He explained to me as we walked away that if boys and girls bound together by kinship ties were allowed to exercise violence, such behavior might become a habit. Then how could they go on living in the same village, where, as adults, they would of necessity be mutually dependent? "Brothers may sometimes be irritable with each other—that's to be expected," he concluded. "But severe breaches cannot be permitted, and quarrels must be stopped before they become serious. Grown-up brothers are the village defense as warriors, and certainly this would be impossible without full trust." Children who do not listen to the warnings may be thrashed, not once but several times.

Technical Education

Little girls are absorbed into the social system earlier than their brothers. Perhaps they are by nature more compliant, but probably the mother's demands upon them are more urgent. During the early morning and evening, women are faced with a multitude of pressing jobs, and it is a great help to have somebody mind the baby for a few minutes, fetch a hot coal from the neighbor's to kindle a fire, do the washing up, or fill the water bottles. They call upon a daughter instead of a son, partly because tasks of this kind are looked upon as the concern of females rather than males, partly because a daughter is more likely to

---

[1] H. I. Hogbin, 1958, has a photograph (facing p. 54) of a group of Longgu children offering bride price in a wedding game.

be close at hand whereas a son may be away at the other end of the village or swimming off the reef with his agemates. Another important consideration is that women's work is focused on the hearth, but men perform the bulk of their toil at a distance, in the forest or out at sea. A father would therefore find a small boy, who would have to be watched, something of a nuisance. The result is that he delays taking his sons with him till they are older.

Girls go to the gardens regularly with their mother from about the age of eight. They cannot yet wield the heavy digging stick or bush knife, but they assist in collecting the rubbish before planting begins, in piling up the earth, and weeding. Boys start accompanying their father some two or three years later, when they help with the clearing, fetch lianas to tie up the saplings that form the fence, and cut up the seed yams. The men may also allocate plots to their sons and speak of the growing yams as their own harvest. The services of a youngster are of economic value from the time that he is pubescent, but he is not expected to take gardening really seriously until after he returns from the plantation and is thinking of marriage. By then he is conscious of his rights and privileges as a member of his clan and knows where the clan blocks of land are located. As a rule, he can also explain a little about the varieties of yams and taro and the types of soil best suited to each.

At about eight a boy begins to go along with his father or uncles when the men set out in the evening with their lines to catch fish from the shore or on the reef. They make a small rod for him, show him how to bait his hook, and tell him about the different species of fish—where they are to be found, which are good to eat, which are poisonous. At the age of ten the boy makes an occasional fishing excursion in a canoe. To start with, he sits in the center of the canoe and watchs, perhaps baiting the hooks and removing the catch; but soon he takes part with the rest. In less than a year he is a useful crew member and expert in steering and generally handling the craft. At the same time, I have seen youths under the age of sixteen out at sea by themselves. Often they are eager to go before this, but the elders are unwilling to give permission lest they endanger themselves or the canoe.

Most fathers have allocated at least one pig to the son by the time he is about eight; moreover, they insist that he accept the full obligation to gather and husk coconuts each day so that the animal can be fed in the evening. Usually the child is at first keenly interested, but after a time he may have to be scolded severely to make him attend to his duty. The father kills the animal or gives it away when the need arises, but always makes a great show of consulting the boy first and explaining the circumstances of the decision. Many a boy makes a pet of his own pig and grieves when it is taken from him.

An amusing incident took place in Riani's household after he had given his middle son a first pig. The youngest in the family, Lulua, a child of seven, was envious of his two elder brothers and begged his father to give him an animal. Riani pointed out that he had none left, but promised to set one aside the next time a sow farrowed. Lulua then went to his cousin Raisi, who, though slightly younger, had already received a piglet from his father. "Raisi, give me that," he demanded. "You are my younger brother, and it would be wrong for you to refuse." Raisi dutifully did as he was told, and Lulua went home with the pig in his arms. Riani made him put it in a sty and three days later begged Raisi's father to take it back. Lulua went looking for it, but Raisi, coached by his parents, told him that it had been sold to a man from Malaita.

Older children are spurred on mainly by praise for good behavior and by favorable comparisons with others. "Good, that's what I like to see," said one man when his twelve-year-old son finished planting a plot of yams. "My boy, persevere, and when you're old enough all the elders in the village will be arguing with one another about which of them is to have you as a husband for his daughter or niece."

Beatings are now a thing of the past. It is thought to be both indecorous and dangerous for adults to strike a youth or adolescent girl: he or she might now retaliate, if not with blows, then perhaps by the destruction of valuable property. Parents, and uncles and aunts as well, do not hesitate, however, to relieve their feelings by pouring out the filthiest abuse, which the boy or girl returns in kind. The worst verbal matches of this kind that I witnessed were all between close kinsmen of different generations—parents and teen-age sons and daughters, or uncles and aunts (patrilateral and matrilateral) and teen-age nephews and nieces. I can give here only the roughest indication of the sort of remarks uttered; the actual expressions were too crude for publication even in an anthropological series. "Defecate in your own loincloth," shouted Tanggu when his son annoyed him. "Oh, go and copulate with feces," the lad replied. "You're nothing but a lump of woman's excrement," another man screamed at his sister's son, an insult that met the response, "Choke yourself with a bowl full of urine." The people standing nearby make clucking noises in disapproval, but are neither shocked nor horrified. "A blow from the tongue is better than a swipe with a clenched fist," they said to me.

Tensions between members of the parent and the child generations are a commonplace of social life in all parts of the world. There are many reasons why this is so. The father and uncles may be jealous of their successors and unwilling to accept a reminder of their failing powers; and, correspondingly, the sons and nephews may chafe under criticism and correction. The bad language of the Longgu folk provides a safety valve for the pent-up irritations. In societies that do not offer such a harmless outlet, the strains of the relationships can lead to open rebellion.

I take this opportunity to put forward the hypothesis that, if bitter struggles regularly take place between the generations, then contemporaries—brothers particularly—in order to present a united front, will tend to smother their own rivalries. But I doubt whether the converse is valid: that manifest hostility between those of the same age group is always accompanied by harmony between old and young.

4

Getting a Living

THE GUADALCANAL YEAR is dominated by two winds, the southeast trade from early June to September and the northwest monsoon from late November to April. At the end of each season and before the next begins, there is an interval of calm and variable winds. Both major divisions might be described as wet, but during that of the trade wind even more rain falls than during the monsoon. The rhythm of work is in consequence not very marked, and most tasks are carried on with nearly the same intensity in March or in September, in June or December.

Life is busiest at the time of the full moon, when the extra light stretches the day by several hours. It is therefore surprising that no names should be available for either the successive nights or the months. When thinking ahead, the natives mostly rely on the sequence provided by the changes in certain botanical species. *Aikopi* is the period of the flowering of one of the shrubs, *Mburu* that of the flowering of a grass, *Alosuisui* that of the flowering of a creeper, *Rara* that of the fruiting of a forest tree, and so on. These are checked against the prevailing winds, the Canarium-almond harvest (which comes at the opening of the monsoon), and the evening positions of the constellations Pleiades and Orion.

Horticulture

Cultivation is by the slash-and-burn method. The ground is cleared, the timber destroyed, and two or sometimes three crops planted one after the other. The area is then abandoned for a period of ten years or more.

Yams, taro, and sweet potatoes are grown month by month, and at any given moment each householder has from four to six gardens at different stages. Yams, however, do a little better when sown during the height of the trade-wind season. Most persons plan therefore to have a few more plots prepared then. The tubers are ready at the tail end of the monsoon, a period known as *Walisi*.

Probably everyone makes an occasional small garden by himself, but in general the subclan members from the hamlet collaborate. They discuss the matter in the clubhouse during the evening and decide on which area and when they will begin. One or more of their number may at this particular time not wish to join in, perhaps on account of other commitments, perhaps because of a temporary shortage of seed yams, taro suckers, or sweet-potato runners, but the rest make appropriate arrangements. The older men take some of their young uterine nephews as helpers and also expect any married son living nearby to accompany them. Sometimes they also invite other relatives, including affines. Adult guests have to lend a hand in the clearing and fencing and are then allocated a section, which, of course, reverts back to the clan as soon as the last crop has been gathered in.

The oldest active man in the subclan is in charge; should leadership in any of the tasks be necessary, he directs the operations. He selects the patch to be used with reference to such factors as the presence of certain shrubs and the girth of the trees. The first are regarded as indicators of the quality of the soil, the second as fixing the length of time that the ground has lain fallow. He orders the party to cut the brushwood, and later they fell the bigger timber. The rubbish dries out and is burned within a few weeks.

So far the males alone have been engaged in cultivation. The women now go along also to scatter the ashes over the soil and remove any further growth. In the meantime the men construct a stout fence around the block.

In the next stage the leader divides the clearing into plots, one for every household. The men mark the borders with flimsy palisades, then cut the plots into strips, one for every dependent. This final subdivision, although of little practical significance, serves to demonstrate the size of the garden, information that cannot otherwise be obtained in a community that lacks a means of measuring length or area.

Yams always form the first main crop. The men make a series of holes with a digging stick; later they and the women cut the seed tubers into pieces, each with an eye, which all go together and plant. After a lapse of some weeks the women make up a gang of weeders to clear the patch. Each may stick to her own household plot, but more frequently they combine and go from end to end in one long line. A few more weeks and the men have another turn. They cut stakes and fix them for the yam vines to climb on. Often, too, they build a shed or two to serve as shelter for any family that may wish to stay for a couple of days. Subsequently they fix shelves just below the roof so that the ripened yams can be stored, especially those that are picked out for seed. The women remove the weeds on one further occasion, and later on they dig up the tubers. The small ones are easily extracted, but harvesting the larger varieties, even though they weigh only a few pounds, is a tedious job demanding half an hour or more of scooping the earth around each one. (The 10-feet-long monster tubers, common in parts of New Guinea and in the Trobriands, are unknown in the Solomons.)

In addition to yams, each householder has patches of green vegetables and tobacco and also a few banana trees. The women plant and care for the green vegetables and tobacco; women and men plant bananas, and the men cut down the bunches of ripe fruit and carry them home. The tobacco leaves are first spread out in the sun, usually by the men, and then transferred to a shelf over the cooking fire. When fully matured they are rolled into bundles, each weighing about 4 pounds. A smoker cuts off a small wedge and rubs it in his palms before filling his pipe. (Nowadays the pipes are of Western manufacture, but formerly they were made from a shell and a reed.)

Depending on the type of soil, the second crop is either taro or sweet potatoes. If taro has been chosen, the women bring along suckers from an old garden, and the members of both sexes combine to plant them. As before, the women do the weeding and harvesting. By this time the fences are probably falling into disrepair, and the subclan leader has to arrange with the men for their renovation.

The third crop, if the people decide to have one, is almost always sweet potatoes. Men and women cut shoots off the plants in another garden and dig one end of each shoot into the earth. The ripening tubers attract the pigs even more than do yams and taro, and the fence must now be regularly inspected and, if need be, strengthened.

The men carry all the very heavy loads, as, for example, when extra supplies have to be brought in for a feast; but it is women's work to take the daily food home from the cultivations. They put the yams, taro, or sweet potatoes into a flat basket, which they lift onto a woven ring of cane placed on top of the head. A weight of 80 pounds is not regarded as too heavy a load; and I have never seen anything fall.

Fishing

Constructing a plank canoe is a difficult undertaking, and only a few men possess the necessary skill. Such experts are prepared to work for a close relative without return, but from others they expect payment in strings of shell discs or pigs and yams. They receive many requests, and nearly all the senior householders own a small fishing craft capable of holding three or four people.

In offshore fishing a man may go out by himself, but more frequently takes a couple of companions, perhaps his sons or nephews, perhaps some other near kinsmen or an affine. A certain amount of borrowing takes place, though only between people living fairly near to one another. The owner of the craft, or, if he is staying at home, the senior person present, sits in the bow and directs the crew to the reef he considers most promising. The man at the stern steers, but most of the physical work is done by the man in the middle. He paddles, bails out the water that washes over the gunwale, and keeps the canoe steady when his companions have a tug at their lines. By day the usual methods of fishing are with baited hooks or with lures, but at night one member of the crew waves a coconut-leaf flare rhythmically up and down, and the rest use either spears or nets.

Bonito fishing is one of the few seasonal activities, not on account of the migration of the fish, but because they must be sought in the passage separating Guadalcanal and the Malaita Islands, a stretch of water that provides no shelter from monsoonal gales, which are sometimes severe. A single bonito may weigh as much as 30 pounds. The flesh is a great delicacy, and in the past its consumption was accompanied by a good deal of ritual. In those days, too, the father always inaugurated an expedition for all the kinsfolk when he thought his son old enough to first accompany him bonito fishing.

On special occasions, as when a feast is planned, groups of men, headed by the seniors of the subclan, collect fish on the fringing reefs. They fasten scores of split coconut leaves end to end to make a curtain-like construction 80 yards or more long. Holding this in front of them, they wade into the water and encircle any shoal there may be. The youths leap into the middle with nets and spears and catch as many fish as possible.

Formerly seine fishing was practiced, but the younger generation failed to acquire the accompanying magical spells, and the nets were never renewed.

Except in reef fishing, which is carried out for a specific purpose, the catch is regarded as the property of the owner of the canoe or the man who borrowed it from the owner. If the haul is small he bids the paddlers take the craft to a beach outside the village, and here they roast the fish and eat them straight away without vegetables. He divides larger hauls more or less evenly, but takes the biggest share himself in order to pass on a little to the expert responsible for fashioning the canoe in the first place. Each man takes his portion home for the family larder.

House Construction

Building is the most onerous of the ordinary tasks. The actual work in putting up an average dwelling takes over 100 man-days, and, in addition, the owner has to feed the laborers each day and, at the end, reward them with a feast. The job is spread over four or five weeks; there are several intervals so that those engaged can keep up with their other duties.

As usual, the householder discusses the matter with his near kinsmen from the hamlet and outside. These men now search in the forest for trees suitable for the posts and ridge pole, and on the day agreed upon, they go and cut them down. Next they spread word of their work around the village and perhaps to some of the man's relatives living elsewhere. Again a convenient day is chosen, and several gangs set out to haul the logs to shore and float them to the village.

The owner of the house has already requested an expert in building,

DOMESTIC TASKS · 45

preferably a close relative or someone married to a close relative, to superintend operations. This man starts the work as soon as he can spare the time, and the assembly of kinsfolk, acting under his orders, set the posts in the ground.

Within a few days the menfolk return to the forest once more to cut timber for the beams, purlins, and rafters. These they also bring to the village and, directed by an expert, lash them into place.

Collecting the leaf from ivory-nut palms (a type of sago) is the next job. The people make for the swamps, hack leaves from the palms, cut off the leaflets, tie these into huge bundles, and bring them in. Meantime others have been gathering canes, which they trim to a length of about 4 feet. The men now choose a sunny day to prepare the thatch. They bend the leaflets over the canes and skewer them in place with the midrib previously split off, thus producing a sheet like a large tile. These are spread out to dry for two or three days, then carefully gathered into heaps toward the second or third evening.

Before the sheets can be tied to the rafters, a scaffolding has to be built inside the posts to support the workers. This demands still more timber from the forest. Generally the thatch can be finished in a day, though the tighter the canes are packed—and therefore the thicker the leaf—the longer the roof will last.

Next come the walls. The uprights are driven into the ground first, then the split saplings fastened between them with strips of tough liana.

So far the women have played no part in the building. On each working day, however, they cook dishes of food, which they bring over to the men when the allotted task is completed. The wives and daughters of the hamlet work together under the instruction of either their senior or the spouse of the house owner; but other women, especially the owner's sisters, make a considerable contribution. The men also leave the gathering of the pebbles that are scattered on the floor and the weaving of the bed mats to the females.

A week or two after the house has been occupied the owner entertains all his helpers with a feast. I shall describe this in a later chapter.

Domestic Tasks

Usually the children are awake first and begin tugging at their still-sleeping parents soon after dawn. The men stir themselves and make their way to the beach, where some may take a cool bath. The women sweep the house and then blow up the fire. If no live embers from the night before remain, one of the older girls begs some from a neighbor. As soon as the flames appear the housewife proceeds to warm up the vegetables left over from the previous evening's meal. She cooks fresh food only when the husband has been out during the night and has caught fish. On such mornings she roasts a few yams and offers some to everybody. Often the men decline to eat anything and wait for a snack at midday.

Afterwards the woman places anything that has still not been consumed in baskets. Children who are staying at home help themselves as often as they feel hungry; but the youths, girls, and adults put their shares of food in a hand-bag, which they carry with them to their place of work—the garden, the forest, or the canoe. This food is eaten cold, generally with the fluid from a green coconut.

The only formal meal of the day is supper, which the woman aims to have ready shortly before nightfall. In this latitude there is little variation in the length of the day, and the sun always sets at approximately six o'clock. Suppertime is therefore around a quarter to six. If the man of the house is still absent, perhaps fishing or in the forest, his wife sets aside a share and reheats it on his return.

Yams, taro, or sweet potatoes are always served and, if it is available, fish: should it not be, then greens or roasted nuts have to suffice. Unlike the natives of New Guinea, those of the Solomons have no clay cooking pots, and the root vegetables have to be cooked in an oven. The woman piles stones on the fire to become red hot. Meantime she scrubs the yams, or, if taro or sweet potatoes are being used, she removes their skin. She then puts half the hot stones in a depression in the ground, covers them with green banana leaves, adds the roots, covers these also with leaves, piles on the rest of the stones, and finally places a thick pad of still more banana leaves over the top. Everything should be done at the end of about an hour and a half, but as clocks are lacking she has to guess at the interval.

The woman washes the greens, if need be removes the fibrous stems, and places the leaves in a tall wooden bowl about 2 feet high. She adds a little salt water and a little fresh water, then pushes a few very hot stones into the middle with a pair of bamboo tongs. A pad of leaves goes on top, but every few minutes this comes off to enable her to change the place of the stones. While this food is steaming she grates a coconut and squeezes out the white milk. This she pours over the top, with a little more water, before serving the dish.

Cooking with Canarium almonds demands more effort. In one recipe the yams, taro, or sweet potatoes are first grated raw, and the pulp is spread on leaves, wrapped up, and put in the oven in the usual way. The next step is to pound the almonds in a mortar with a small quantity of water. The water and oil are poured off into a wooden dish, and the cooked pulp is mixed in the mortar with the pounded nuts. Finally the oil and water go back on the top.

In another method the cook scoops a hole in the center of the raw yams or sweet potatoes (taro will not do) and fills this hole with almond paste before baking. Today the Christians frequently serve this dish on Sunday evenings, when religious restrictions prevent the men from fishing.

Two other dishes are reserved for feasts and similar occasions, as when visitors come or a woman wishes to give her husband a treat. For the first a number of yams are peeled and boiled in a wooden bowl by means of hot stones. The latter have to be replaced several times, and two hours or more pass before the yam flesh is sufficiently tender for mashing with a paddle-shaped implement. The paste is then mixed to a thick cream with the addition of salt water and the white milk from grated coconuts. Sweet potatoes may be used instead of yams;

when this is done, the cook achieves a decorative effect by having alternate layers, or separate bowls, of the white, yellow, and purple varieties.

In the second of the special dishes, grated raw yams or sweet potatoes are mixed with pounded almonds or white coconut milk. Lumps, each weighing about 2 pounds, are then spread on banana leaves, wrapped up, and put in the oven.

Pigs, as was mentioned, are prepared only for feasts, and the whole process is carried out by men. They kill the animal either by clubbing it on the head or by strangling it, after which it is tied to a pole and singed thoroughly on an open fire. A skilled butcher carves the carcass into joints, which are cooked in the oven with hot stones in the usual way.

The woman calls the children into the house for their evening meal and makes them sit down. Each may choose a seat on his own bed if she has enough wooden dishes to give them one apiece; if not, they gather in a circle near her and eat with a coconut-shell spoon from a couple of large bowls. She removes any bones from the fish that she offers to the small boys and girls but is content with warning those who are older to be careful. The husband may also join in, should he be at home; otherwise she sets his food aside till he is ready. Generally she waits till everybody else is fed before eating anything herself.

Both parents train their offspring in the etiquette of eating. They insist that each should sit facing the center of the house to avoid any suspicion of hoarding titbits. Gobbling food is strongly condemned, but it is not considered impolite to belch or smack the lips. Children are also told that, except when in the houses of their uncles or aunts, they must never ask for food; further, if given something, they are told that they should either eat it all up or else make an excuse for having left a piece and offer this to another person in the house.

Trade

The resources of the area are by island standards rich, and the natives have little difficulty in producing a surplus of pigs, vegetables, and tobacco. The first two go mainly to the people of Langalanga Lagoon off the west coast of Malaita. These folk live on tiny islets built of coral blocks brought up one by one from the sea floor, and as in such confined quarters there is no room to plant gardens or keep animals, all food except fish must be obtained elsewhere. In return, the Langalanga natives offer strings of shell discs. For some reason they have no interest in the tobacco, but this is in demand on the northern end of San Cristoval Island, where the villagers have stocks of porpoise teeth for exchange.

The Longgu and their neighbors keep most of the strings of discs and porpoise teeth, but have to give some away in order to acquire from within Guadalcanal itself or from other islands such items as dog's teeth, extra tobacco, carved wooden food bowls, wicker shields, large seagoing canoes, and ornaments made from clamshell and turtleshell.

Before discussing the exchanges in detail I must first say a little more about the strings of discs. Langalanga is the mint for this type of currency. The natives work with three kinds of shell: the red-lipped Spondylus, a white mollusk, and a black mussel. They break these into pieces of approximately the right size, stick them into slabs of wood by means of a thick paste, and grind them smooth on a sandstone block. Next they bore a hole in the center, round off and polish the edges. The discs that pass inspection are then strung on tough pandanus cords. The people from the various parts of the Solomons differ in their preferences regarding the number of strings bound together, their length, and the shade and size of the discs. Around Longgu, the villagers like a preponderance of raspberry-pink Spondylus, each disc to be about three eighths of an inch in diameter. As indicated, these must be done up in sets consisting of two, three, four, five, and six pairs, each one fathom long. But the Longgu villagers, because of their trade with other places, have to take different kinds of strings. At Marau, on the eastern tip of Guadalcanal, the natives insist on elaborately worked belts (*kariavara*) made from smaller, pinker discs, and the residents of the interior favor white discs in preference to pink ones.

The chief functions of the discs and teeth are ceremonial. We have seen that they form a large part of the bride price; and they are also given as compensation for injuries and as a reward to allies after a victory. But on festive occasions, the strings of discs may be worn as shoulder straps, and the teeth, set in webbing, sometimes serve as collars. The Longgu headman owned the most magnificent of these that I saw. It was a prize specimen consisting of seven rows, each made up of 90 dog's teeth.

Europeans and natives alike refer to the valuables as "island money," an expression that is misleading because it implies a purely economic use. Certainly each of the objects can be given an equivalent in dollar values: a Marau belt is held to be worth at least 28 dollars (10 pounds sterling), an ordinary fathom of discs 70 cents (5 shillings), 2 dog's teeth 14 cents (1 shilling), and 10 porpoise teeth 14 cents (1 shilling). Yet the people will sell for cash only in exceptional circumstances, as when they cannot pay their head tax. It is also true that the valuables serve as a medium of exchange, as a store of value, and as a unit of account, though here the field is highly restricted. They are a liquid asset in that they can be readily turned into wooden bowls or shields or canoes; at the same time, nobody ever thinks of the worth of his dwelling or garden in terms of these valuables or ever attempts to purchase buildings or cultivations with them. Further, discs and teeth are not interchangeable. A fathom of discs, or 10 dog's teeth, or 50 porpoise teeth may all be assumed to have a market value of 70 cents (5 shillings), but a fathom of discs cannot be equated with either 10 dog's teeth or 50 porpoise teeth. Each traditional transaction requires its own kind of objects—discs alone, dog's teeth alone, porpoise teeth alone, or, as in a bride price, some of all three in a fixed proportion.

From time to time the discs must be restrung, but in themselves they are practically everlasting. This also applies to the teeth. A senior man, to establish his importance, may ostentatiously bury some of his valuables, but until very recently more and more went into circulation each year.[1] New and old were equally esteemed, and these natives, unlike many Melanesians, do not follow up the history of really ancient pieces or regard them as heirlooms. I suspect therefore that gradual inflation may have occurred. The middle-aged men confirm that they have to lay out rather more than their fathers did for the same type of goods, but deny that their own demands in respect to pigs and vegetables have increased.

Trade is based on partnerships between individuals, who not only make the exchanges but also provide mutual protection and hospitality. Thus each householder has at least one partner in every community with which his own is on visiting terms. These men he refers to as his *u'undu,* an expression he explains by saying that they and he, though not in fact kin, are "the same as brothers." The relationships are usually inherited from father to son or from uncle to nephew. (Formerly our concept of "friend" was unknown, but today, in the conditions of the plantation, laborers use *u'undu* for unrelated companions coming from widely separated districts.)

The Langalanga natives are the greatest voyagers of the area. When one of their canoes reaches Longgu and has been properly beached, each member of the crew carries his belongings to the house of his partner, who immediately makes him welcome. He may at once present his host with such strings of discs as he has brought, or he may delay till just before departure. He does not say outright what he wishes to take back, but within a day or two he begins dropping hints. He may praise the appearance of a particularly fat pig, or call attention to a couple of smaller animals as likely to make succulent pork, or speak of the excellent quality of the local yams or sweet potatoes. A host who does not at the moment have the right thing available must obtain it from a kinsman. If he is lucky, somebody in need of valuables, possibly for an unexpected wedding, will be eager to oblige. The visitor remains discreetly in the background and plays no part in the negotiations.

After about a week the party fixes the day for the journey home. The hosts catch the pigs to be in readiness and bring in the vegetables from the gardens. The cargo is stowed, good-byes are said, and the canoes paddle away.

It is difficult to say how many pigs are exported annually, but two or three fleets come across in every twelve-month period, and I have seen one fleet carry as many as twenty.

The Guadalcanal natives do not go to Langalanga nearly as often, partly because they decline to think of themselves as long-distance sailors, partly because their drive to acquire valuables is less urgent than that of their partners to acquire food. The expeditions always consist of from three to half a dozen canoes, a survival of the time when the voyagers might have been forced to defend themselves from hostile attack. The proceedings are the same as those just described, except that in this case the Guadalcanal guests bring the supplies and drop hints about their requirements. They may want the customary strings,

---

[1] See C. S. Belshaw, 1950, p. 178.

the belts admired at Marau, or some white discs. A man who is owed valuables may make the trip empty-handed in expectation of having the debt speedily settled, a hope that is seldom disappointed.

Occasionally on the way back, the party makes a detour to San Cristoval. Here they unload tobacco and take porpoise teeth aboard. The San Cristoval villagers, although they regularly go to Malaita and to the extreme eastern end of Guadalcanal, do not stop off in Longgu.

The large canoes needed for overseas voyages are never immediately available; they have to be constructed, and a slightly different procedure is therefore necessary to procure them. The initiative rests with the leading elder of one of the subclans. As a rule, he solicits contributions from the other members, and when enough has been accumulated he goes either to Marau or to Florida Island, depending on where he has the best contacts. He presents the valuables to his partner and indicates what sort of craft interests him. After the work is finished, the partner brings the canoe over with the help of a skeleton crew, or he may send word for the man to come and fetch it.

Trade also takes place between the dwellers in the mountains and those on the coast of Guadalcanal. The former are eager to have discs, porpoise teeth, coconuts, lime, and salt, and they are prepared to give their particular special- ities. Those living behind Longgu offer tobacco and dog's teeth; those behind Ruavatu, some 15 miles to the west, carved wooden food bowls; and those be- hind Berande, further west again, woven-wicker shields. The Longgu thus be- come the distributors of dog's teeth, the Ruavatu of bowls, and the Berande of shields. In the same way the natives of Florida are the middlemen for the clam- shell and turtleshell ornaments manufactured on Ysabel Island to the north.

Prices may have increased over the generations, as has been suggested, but haggling is unknown, and from year to year no change is apparent. For a pig, depending on the size, a Langalanga native presents from 30 to 50 fathom- length strings of ordinary diameter (or 1 Marau belt and 10 strings). Such a gift satisfies the Longgu native, and he does not think he ought to receive more. The cost of the smallest overseas canoe is 40 strings (or 1 Marau belt), 100 dog's teeth, and 100 porpoise teeth. The cost of the largest is exactly three times as much. Ten wooden serving bowls are worth 4 strings, 10 dog's teeth, and 10 porpoise teeth; a shield is worth 6 strings; and an Ysabel ornament 8 strings. For none of these items is cash acceptable. Sometimes the reimbursement may be delayed, but a man always pays up in the end. He knows that a defaulter's reputation suffers, that he would be barred from future exchanges, and that he would risk having sorcery performed against him.

One further point must be mentioned. Middlemen make no profit. They enter into the transaction because it provides them with an excuse for engaging in social intercourse with peoples whom they would otherwise see only on very rare occasions.

5

Conflict

ESIDENTS OF THE SAME VILLAGE live in harmony most of the time. They themselves attribute the prevailing concord to three factors—training, kinship, and mutual dependence. They point out that they are taught in childhood to refrain from quarreling, that disloyalty to a relative would be wrong, and that nobody can afford to forego the help of his fellows. If a man should harbor a grievance against a neighbor, instead of causing an open rupture, he usually resorts to sorcery behind closed doors. He has no compunction about inflicting slight misfortunes, but would not wish the victim to become aware of what was going on and so have an excuse for anger, and would still less want him to die and leave the community short of an essential worker—and in olden days of a warrior. Accordingly, he chooses black magic of the type that is supposed to result in a minor illness.

Each of the various ailments has an associated system of magic, with a set of rites to induce the complaint and another set to cure it. Every householder owns one or more systems, and, although the procedures are his personal property and carefully guarded for ultimate transmission to his heirs, he freely admits the fact of his knowledge. Thus the villagers are able to indicate which of their fellows can produce and cure colds, which toothaches, which headaches, which biliousness, which diarrhea, which infected cuts, and so forth; moreover, they assume that anybody who has been injured will retaliate by bewitching the man thought to be at fault.

The islands are unhealthy, and there is much disease. Hence the sorcerer, even if he has to wait months, always has the satisfaction in the end of seeing the culprit take to his bed. It is true that magic carried out for one disorder may appear to have led to something else, but this is readily explained away. Another offended party may have accomplished his magic first, or the spells could have been recited inaccurately, or perhaps the magic worked itself out in an unaccustomed manner.

A person who becomes ill takes for granted that he must have been bewitched but makes no effort to discover the sorcerer responsible. Indeed, even if rites had been performed, the utmost secrecy would have been preserved and real evidence could scarcely be forthcoming. The usual course is to seek the aid of one of the men who know the curative rites for the disease. As a rule, the patient's natural resistance triumphs within a few days, and he recovers. Once again, then, the magic seems to be effective. Should he fail to respond, his relatives conclude that some other forces are at work, and they try a different remedy.

Disputes

The rare breaches of peace that occur can be separated into two categories: those in which men of a single subclan are concerned and those in which the parties belong to different subclans. I shall deal with the disputes in that order.

The subclan forms a residential unit, a property-holding unit, and a unit of economic cooperation for such everyday tasks as gardening, fishing, trading, and repairing buildings and equipment. The members, despite their many shared interests, are apt to grow weary of the constant calls for assistance, always from the same individuals, and from time to time tempers become frayed. It is not unknown for neighbors to forget themselves to the extent that they will abuse one another, and very occasionally they may even start fighting for reasons they afterwards admit were trivial. When this happens, the rest of the occupants of the hamlet refrain from taking sides. They concentrate instead on restoring order. The older men, who are looked upon as maternal uncles, keep yelling, "Stop, you two; you should be ashamed of yourselves," while the more agile contemporaries of the antagonists, all of whom are classified as brothers, rush in and try to drag the pair apart. Eventually they succeed and lead each contestant away and try to calm him down. Within a day or two collaboration is going on as before, and the incident is apparently forgotten. "A person never nourishes anger against his brother for long," it is explained. "He looks to him every day for support—each is like an extra hand for the other." If blows have been struck or if the insults were really wounding, reconciliation takes place before the subclan seniors and is accompanied by an exchange of ten or more strings of discs.

Trouble between men from two subclans, especially if these are parts of different clans, may bring about a bigger upset. When the injured person feels that his wrongs are too grievous for adequate redress by means of disease sorcery he gathers the members of his own and his father's subclans and also his brothers-in-law and makes a public demand for satisfaction. They set out together for the hamlet of the offender and say loudly what they think of him, finishing up with a claim for compensation. The members of the offender's subclan, of his father's subclan, and his brothers-in-law rally to his side and defend him to the best of their ability. An argument develops, but as a rule all present have been careful to leave their weapons at home lest, in the heat of the moment, they should be tempted to start a battle. If the defendant ultimately says he is sorry, or either from his own resources or through loans produces a reasonable amount of valuables, all is well again, and the accusers retire. But he may not have enough valuables, or the sum asked for may be out of all proportion to the damages inflicted, or there may be extenuating circumstances, or the charge may be without foundation. As soon as it becomes plain that a satisfactory conclusion is unlikely and that brawling is imminent, the village headman intervenes. He takes his spears, or sends an armed representative, and threatens the crowd with all sorts of dire penalties if they do not disperse. He has no real authority, but the people respect him and feel that they can obey without losing face.

Later, usually after a few days' interval to allow the participants to simmer down, the headman calls a village meeting (*ndetei*) to investigate the case. The whole population assembles, but, apart from those directly implicated, the elders do the talking. The headman acts as a sort of chairman, though proceedings are informal, and nothing is ever put to a vote. He begins by outlining the situation as he knows it, then calls upon the parties to give an account of themselves. The seniors ask questions and make suggestions, and when the evidence has been heard they give their considered opinion. If it appears that the defendant is innocent, especially if he swears that he is blameless, they advise an exchange of valuables. (The oath may take one of three forms, but in no case is it believed that a lie will be followed by unpleasant consequences supernaturally induced. The man may say, "If I am not speaking the truth I will go in at the anus of my accuser and climb till I emerge at his mouth"; or "If I am not speaking the truth I will eat my accuser's excrement"; or "If I am not speaking the truth I will eat my mother's excrement.") But if the defendant seems to be guilty the seniors determine what, in the light of precedents, he ought to pay. The headman directs their deliberations and tries to secure a unanimous verdict. Should he fail, he adjourns the assembly for a week or two, hoping that by that time the villagers who have close ties with both men will have used their influence to secure an acceptable compromise.

Similar meetings are held to settle civil disputes. The plaintiff requests the headman to have the matter investigated, and judgment is based on the facts elicited by the elders.

Clearly, the headman has an important part to play, and there can be no doubt that he exercises a strong influence. Yet he commands less often than he persuades, and his sway over the community depends on the fact that he represents the voice of popular opinion. In the past, when rival contenders for the office might have been waiting to displace him, the people would have removed him had he been unduly sympathetic toward his near kinsmen. He had no personal bodyguard, and rebellion therefore presented no difficulties, especially when every person was a trained warrior.

Causes of Trouble

The principal offense is adultery. It is said that a man who catches his wife's lover *in flagrante* has the right to kill him on the spot, but the cases cited all relate to the past, long before the oldest men living today had been born. At present, compensation of one *ndovu* is expected (40 strings, 40 dog's teeth, and 100 porpoise teeth). The husband always beats his erring spouse and is free to take her back or divorce her.

Persuading a married woman to elope is more serious, and the penalty is not only an extra half *ndovu* for the husband but also valuables for her relatives to recompense them for the loss of the bride price that they now have to return. During my stay in Longgu in 1933, the man Kapini ran off with the wife of Avata. The pair fled to some of Kapini's relatives, who were also his fellow clansmen, living in Nangali, and it was with these folk that the pair eventually set up a household. Avata's first reaction was to spear as many of Kapini's pigs as he could lay hands on. No one ventured to touch them, and the carcasses rotted. Later, he threatened to burn down Kapini's house in Longgu, but relatives dissuaded him. Then he announced what is known as a *noha,* a solemn declaration that so long as he lived he would never speak to Kapini, eat with him, or look him in the face. When I returned ten years later, though I saw them on a couple of occasions in the same gathering, the taboo was still in operation.

Other misdeeds include theft and surreptitiously killing other people's pigs. Stealing from houses almost never occurs, doubtless, among other reasons, because the property would soon be recognized and the guilt plain for all to see. Even gardens are seldom interfered with, though very occasionally a man who is short of seed yams helps himself from the wrong storehouse, a building that is invariably located in the cultivations. Tracing the thief is difficult, but, once identified, he is made to hand over discs and teeth to cover both the value of the goods and the inconvenience resulting from their loss.

Sometimes a hunter spears a village pig in the forest under the misapprehension that it is a wild boar. He ought, on discovering his error, to carry the carcass to the owner and indicate his willingness to pay damages. But he may decide not to confess and instead invite his brothers to a secret feast. Should the owner of the pig find out about this—as he almost always does—the price demanded is twice what the pig would fetch on the open market, "one lot of valuables for the slaughter, one lot for the pork." The same rule applies if a man kills a village pig that has broken into his garden. The blame lies with him for neglecting to keep his fence in good repair, and a claim for the loss of the crop would be dismissed.

A few people are described as "dead to shame," but the average person whose conduct is judged to have been wrong or unworthy feels humiliated and embarrassed. If he is young and as yet has no children to support, he may go away and serve a further term of employment with a European; in cases where he cannot shelve his responsibilities he keeps out of the public eye for a few weeks or months. Disinterested villagers never forget his misdeeds, but, except when angry with him on their own account, they refrain from mentioning them in his presence.

Habitual offenders, individuals who are indifferent to reputation and a good name, are today brought before the magistrate's court and sent to jail.

In the past their unpopularity would sooner or later have led to their being killed. I shall return to them presently.

Most of the civil disputes—and again I emphasize their rare occurrence—relate to the recovery of bride price after divorce. The plaintiff, having failed to secure satisfaction, goes to the headman with a request for a public meeting. The rules are quite definite, and there can be no doubt about the amount that ought to be refunded. The headman has no means of enforcing his decision, but his word, echoing that of the elders, always carries the day.

Everyone knows the subclan that is associated with each plot of ground, and disputes over areas as a whole are unknown. Yet there are times when two groups cannot agree over the precise location of a boundary, one asserting that the line lies on the far side of a particular strip and the other that it lies on the near side. The headman may be forced to give an arbitrary decision if the elders cannot find satisfactory evidence to support either party.

Death Sorcery

The residents of neighboring settlements have fewer opportunities for close contacts, and the chances of conflicts between them are consequently reduced. When the odd case of adultery or pig stealing does crop up, however, there is no intervillage assembly where the differences may be thrashed out.[1] The man bearing the grudge hesitates to tackle the wrongdoer directly because of the risk to himself and his fellows. If a general fight occurred and someone was killed, the bad feeling engendered would preclude future alliances against the attacks of common distant enemies. Sorcery again provides the solution for the problem, though this time one of the lethal types is employed. The injured householder either carries out the rites himself or, if he lacks the skill, invites a companion to do so on his behalf. As before, everything takes place in secret, and the victim is unaware that he has been bewitched. "If he were to be told,"

---

[1] Never in Guadalcanal or in any other part of Melanesia where I have worked have I, myself, heard of a professional peacemaker in disputes between residents of different villages. Fox, who first went to the Solomons shortly after 1900, nevertheless, records in a recent publication that he had been informed of the existence in pre-European times of such an official in the islets of Tae Lagoon, northeastern Malaita. "A boy was chosen and set apart by himself for the rest of his life, and never marry. He was the *manu* and held in great respect, but . . . his only function was to keep the peace. When one [community] threatened war with another, the *manu* was sent to stop the war, and his office was so sacred and he himself held in such honour that . . . it was unthinkable for any to disobey him. The last *manu* died a good many years ago and should have been replaced by some young boy chosen to succeed him, but I believe never was. . . . There were certain signs by which the boy to succeed the *manu* was discovered. Whether the spirit of the dying *manu* entered into his successor I am not sure, but probably this was their belief. His special dress . . . —a garment like an alb, a stole, girdle, and turban, all of native material—was shown to me . . . the *manu* was only a peacemaker, not a ruler." (C. E. Fox, 1962, pp. 115, 116.) Presumably the *manu* fulfilled the same sort of function in intervillage disputes as the headman in village quarrels: he had such prestige that people could yield to his persuasion without loss of reputation. (Cf. the role of the Leopard-Skin Chief of the Nuer of the Sudan: E. E. Evans-Pritchard, 1940, pp. 5, 6, 16, 161 to 174.)

the people say, "there'd be no purpose in holding back from flinging a spear at him."

Death sorcery is of two kinds, *veiveisi'ovi* and *vele*. The former requires that the sorcerer take some of the victim's food remains, recite a spell over them, and fling them into a village shrine. It is said that the spirits avenge the desecration of their sacred place by making the owner of the food ill. The only means of preventing his death is to have the fragments recovered.

Vele is more complicated. A myth relates that it originated on a small islet off the coast of Lau, one of the Russell or Cape Marsh Islands to the west of Guadalcanal. Four Lau fisherman, feeling hungry, decided to pull into the islet for some fresh fruit. One went to look and failed to return. The second followed, then the third. As these did not reappear, the fourth determined to investigate. He found three bodies at the foot of a tree, and that each man had apparently died in the act of taking a bite from a mango. Concluding that the flesh was a deadly poison, he collected a quantity and went home. Today the essential ingredient of *vele* is a small bag containing a portion of these original mangoes or of others since collected from the same tree. Ordinarily the bag will have to be handed down to the sorcerer from his forebears in the female line. Other magic may be taught to the sons; *vele* is transmitted to the brothers or the sisters' sons; it would not work for relatives outside the clan. But it is also possible to buy a *vele* bag and a knowledge of the accompanying ritual from a Lau native. The standard practice then is to try out the magic against a member of the immediate family, preferably a mother or a sister. If this person dies, then the bag must be genuine.

The *vele* sorcerer observes the habits of his victim to discover when he can expect him to be alone. After lying in wait for the man's approach, he catches his eye by emitting a loud whistle. Then he fixes him with a piercing stare and makes circular motions before his face with the bag. Soon the man becomes dizzy and falls into a swoon. The sorcerer forces the clenched teeth open and inserts the bag, and he also cuts a small incision under each fingernail and toenail with a needle-sharp dagger of sting-ray spine. After a minute or two he withdraws the bag and revives the victim with a sharp blow on the elbows and knees. If, at this time, there is a disgusting stench, he knows that he has been successful and that the man will be unaware of what has taken place. A person who has swallowed *vele* poison goes about his tasks as though nothing had happened to him, but after a few hours he suddenly collapses. Unless the sorcery is quickly diagnosed and a magical emetic administered, he is sure to die.

To guard against *veiveisi'ovi* the natives steadfastly refuse to eat in front of anyone to whom they are not closely related, and as a protection against *vele* they bar their doors at night and when out walking try to go in groups. The precautions are taught early and become automatic. Adults show fear only when a fellow villager has just died. Any arrangements made to visit other places are at once cancelled, and for a week or two sorcery is almost the only topic of conversation. It was on such an occasion that I learned that *vele* is powerless against fire and water. The villagers warned me that I should always carry a lighted torch, but that if I forgot to do so and suspected a *vele* sorcerer was lying in wait for me, I could still escape by running into the sea or a river. They also said that if the sorcerer was attacking a woman and, seeing her prostrate before him, attempted to have sexual intercourse, the contents of his bag would at once be neutralized.

A person's identification as a *veiveisi'ovi* or *vele* sorcerer is a measure of his social distinction, and most headmen and numbers of elders are said to possess the necessary knowledge. An ordinary villager has little difficulty, therefore, in finding somebody who will act for him and avenge his wrongs. Yet it is uncertain whether all the men to whom sorcery is ascribed do, in fact, perform it. If they are prominent in community affairs it would be a confession of weakness to admit ignorance. The spells that several individuals taught me would seem to indicate that *veiveisi'ovi* may sometimes be carried out; but I am less willing to accept the bags asserted to contain magical poison as proof of *vele*. The owners might well have made such objects with the deliberate intention of impressing other people. Possibly some of them sincerely believe in their powers, but, if this is so, I am convinced that they must seek out their victims in controlled dreams. I found no shred of evidence suggesting that the bags held a real poison like arsenic or that anybody is capable of killing by hypnosis.

Remedies for Sorcery

We must now see what happens in cases of severe illness. At the onset of the sickness, as was mentioned, the first thing that people think of is disease sorcery. The man submits to curative magic and hopes that all will be well. Should the rites be ineffective and his health deteriorate further, there are two possible explanations. The spirits could be giving a reminder of a neglected sacrifice, or death sorcery could be making an early onslaught. Usually he tries placating the spirits with the promise of a pig, and only as a last resort does he approach a diviner of the particular kind known as *vandivandi* (from *vandi*, to whistle), of whom every village has two or three. These men are supposed to reveal the sort of sorcery used, *veiveisi'ovi* or *vele*, but they do not name the sorcerer.

The patient, or a relative, goes to the diviner's house and explains the symptoms. That evening the specialist spreads a new mat behind his pillow and recites a spell over it. He and the other occupants go outside and wait. After a few minutes a whistling sound appears to come from within—doubtless a trick of ventriloquism. This is the voice of the diviner's spirit familiar, the ghost of his father, calling from the other world. The diviner at once leads the way into the pitch-black house. Should he find that the spirit has recovered the food remains from the sorcerer and left them on the mat, then the disease must be the result of *veiveisi'ovi;* if there is nothing, this is proof of *vele*.

All diviners know the remedy for *veiveisi'ovi*. They murmur a spell over various leaves that have a hot taste, chew them thoroughly, and spit some over the food remains and the rest over the patient. For these services the fee is a few porpoise teeth—provided, that is, the diviner is not a close relative, in which case he acts for nothing.

Discussing the subject in the abstract, people say that *vele* is easily recognizable because the illness begins so suddenly and is accompanied by delirium: in practice, I have known several cases of a *vele* diagnosis in which the person had gone into a gradual decline and never lost consciousness. The remedy, for which another specialist may have to be consulted, consists of a magical potion of leaves and bark that brings on a violent attack of vomiting. The fee is 4 strings of discs.

Should the patient still fail to improve, the efforts continue to recover more of the food remains or to make him go on vomiting, right up to the time he dies.

Death and Vengeance

The infant-mortality rate is high, and when a youngster under the age of about five succumbs the parents are prepared to accept a verdict of "just the sickness of a child," resulting from a ghost's having played with him or her. But all other deaths (including those from what we would call bad luck) are attributed to black magic. The survivors put up with this judgment calmly only if the deceased was thoroughly unpopular—perhaps because of his quarrelsomeness, bad temper, persistent adultery, or habitual thieving. They are then happy to be saved from further embarrassment and may even believe that their own headman has taken pity on them and bewitched the offender. In all other circumstances they demand revenge. Obviously, no action is possible until the sorcerer has been identified, and this is their first aim. They conclude that he must have been operating from a distance or otherwise the remedial measures would have been efficacious. Inevitably suspicion turns toward one or another of the foreign communities that have always been hostile.

On this occasion aid is sought from another kind of diviner, the *to'iai*, who possesses spells that enable him to conjure the dead man's soul into an areca nut. He holds the nut loosely in his hand while he poses a series of questions, all so phrased that they can be answered by a simple negative or affirmative. For "no" the nut remains still; for "yes" it becomes violently agitated and may drag the diviner along for several yards. "Did you die of *vele?*" he asks, "Did the sorcerer come from the coast to the east?" "Did he come from the hills to the north?" "Was he a man of Porombou?" "Or of Komoniboko?" and so on. At length the guilty party is located. More often than not he is the person whose name is already on everyone's lips. The diviner must obviously manipulate the nut, but he is seldom a conscious fraud.

The sort of vengeance to be exacted can now be decided. The village headman, acting at the request of the subclansmen of the dead man, calls a public meeting to talk the matter over. Today, with fighting forbidden, only countersorcery is feasible, though even in the past this was the usual alternative.

Only after an important leader had died were the people prepared to countenance the killing of the sorcerer by open violence. Mourning taboos prevented the relatives of the deceased from taking part in the expedition, and they therefore put a price on the offender's head (*siva*). The subclansmen did a rough calculation of how many valuables they and the other kinsfolk could collect, and the headman then made the announcement. He sent word to the various friendly communities some way off (those close by included too many of the dead man's kinsmen), and within a few weeks one of the communities that was equally at enmity with the settlement of the sorcerer sent a formal acceptance of the *siva* challenge.

These villagers made their resolution for the killing at a general meeting of their own, when they also chose the principal fighter who would be in charge. He might be a headman, but in many places the headman's reputation as a warrior was overshadowed by that of a follower. Whoever was selected worked out the arrangements and gave the orders. His chief preliminary tasks were seeing that the priests offered the sacrifices to the war spirits, that the magicians performed their rites to ensure that the details of the expedition would come off satisfactorily, and that the inexperienced young men taking part in their first raid were aware of the correct dietary and other taboos to be observed.

Once everything was prepared the leader collected the members of his troop, which always included men from neighboring communities, and, during the night, conducted them to the sorcerer's village. Each man carried spears tipped with the carved shinbones of former enemies, an ebony club, and a wicker shield. A few were also expert with a bow and arrow, but this weapon was more commonly used in the interior of the island. As a rule, the assault came as a surprise, and the warriors were able to surround the village without being observed. They waited till dawn, and made a foray as soon as the sleepy inhabitants' began emerging from their houses. The prime objective, of course, was to slay the sorcerer himself, but, though the women and children were safe and persons from the same clan avoided one another, there was no compunction about butchering as many men as possible. Yet the bulk of the population seems to have escaped in the general confusion, and most accounts give the killings that took place on such raids as no more than four or five. This number was increased only on the rare occasions when the villagers knew what was afoot and had posted sentries. These men gave the warning, and there were times when a battle ensued and both sides suffered losses.

If the raid was successful, the warriors cut the heads off all the bodies, and sometimes a leg or an arm as well, to take home with them. They wasted no time in collecting plunder, which would have impeded their progress and made them vulnerable in an ambush.

Upon their return to their own community the members of the war party paused for a few minutes outside the settlement to allow the old men, the women, and the children—especially the boys—to form up for a welcome. They then made a solemn entry, brandishing their spears and singing songs of victory, and set the human trophies on a bench in front of the shrine of a war spirit.

The old folk now encouraged those youths who had been too young to partici-
pate in the raid to strike the victims' heads with clubs and treat them with in-
dignity. Cannibalism was never practiced, but one man told me how, at the age
of fourteen, he had been made to suck blood from the already decaying flesh.
He started vomiting, but his companions told him he was now sure to be a
fierce fighter.

The warriors retired to the clubhouses, where they remained in seclusion for ten days. They were believed to be in a dangerous spiritual condition,
and a passage of time was required before they could take up ordinary work.
During this period they ate vegetables that they themselves had collected in the
night. If they had had anything to do with the rest of the villagers or come into
contact with objects, including food, that others had touched, they would have
become seriously ill. On the eleventh day they offered sacrifices of pigs to the
spirits and then went back to their wives and families.

Meantime, the villagers who had put the price on the sorcerer's head
came to know that the expedition had achieved its aim. The immediate mourners
bathed and shaved for the first time since the death of their kinsman, and the
inhabitants of their own and the surrounding settlements began preparing for
the payment. They collected the strings of discs and the teeth and saw that their
pigs and vegetable supplies were ready.

The date for the handing over of the price was fixed a few days in advance, and that morning the hosts and their assistants cooked enormous quantities of food. Sixty or seventy pigs were not unusual, together with hundreds of
puddings of various kinds. They also erected a long platform about 4 feet above
the ground near the dead man's dwelling. This was to be a sitting place for the
warriors, where they could receive their presents and be generally honored.

At length, about four o'clock in the afternoon, when the sun was no
longer hot, the warriors entered the settlement. They were all fully armed and
richly decorated. In front strode the leader; behind him a younger man carried
the sorcerer's head, which was now in an advanced state of decomposition. It
was placed on a wooden shelf outside the shrine of one of the war spirits. Then,
for a time, the party pranced around the village, hurling spears, destroying property, and boasting about their prowess and courage. The hosts kept out of their
way but threw handfuls of areca nuts, betel pepper, and green drinking-coco-
nuts into corners for their guests to enjoy at leisure.

The headman of the bereaved community now invited the warriors to
ascend the central platform, and for a short time his followers sang songs cele-
brating the achievement. Then he and the senior man of the deceased's subclan
produced the major store of valuables, upwards of 100 *ndovu,* which they offered to the leader of the party, handing it aloft, string after string of discs,
package upon package of teeth. This was the signal for the other men, the non-
uterine relatives and the affines, to come forward with smaller stores of gifts
for the rank and file of the war party.

Next came the distribution of the joints of pork and the puddings. As
with the valuables, these goods went first to the leader. It was his job to dis-

tribute the discs and teeth among the men of his troop and then to divide the food. The bulk he kept for his fellow-campaigners, but he made certain that a portion remained for the hosts. The visitors stayed the night, and set off early in the morning for home, carrying their rewards in baskets on their shoulders.

The residents of the community that had been raided drifted back one by one as soon as they felt they could do so in safety. They buried what was left of the bodies, and now they, too, wanted revenge. No divination was required, for they already knew who the aggressors were. It should be noted that their anger was directed against the attackers themselves, not against the villagers who had encouraged the warriors to set out. Whether countersorcery was appealed to or a price set on the head of the expedition leader depended on the status of the murdered men. If they had been ordinary householders black magic sufficed: if one of them was a headman or in some way important, then a *siva* was declared.

The fact that a group could never confront its enemies openly but was forced by custom to pay others to do its dirty work meant that native warfare in Guadalcanal was different from that in most other parts of Melanesia. Unlike New Guinea, for instance, there were no vendettas, with the two sides raiding each other time after time till so much hatred had been engendered that inevitably a pitched battle took place and the survivors of the vanquished were driven from their lands to take up permanent residence elsewhere, either scattered among relatives or in a new settlement.

The warriors of Guadalcanal, nevertheless, were greatly respected, and a young man had to take part in a campaign and shed blood before he was eligible for marriage or the office of priesthood. Legendary stories relate that, after a long period of peace, villages would deliberately send insults to one another to provoke a fight. I learned of how several generations ago, Sapini, the leading fighter of Aola, told a messenger to inform Balo, a Longgu fighter, that he intended to kill all the Longgu men and seize their wives. Balo replied by sending back a bag of excrement. Sapini marshaled his forces, but Balo was ready for him, and the members of the party would have been slain had not a headman from another village, a person related to both men, begged for their lives. Wars of this kind—if they ever took place, and it is uncertain whether they did—were said to have been followed by a peace-making ceremony (*laka*) at which the two villages, or two sets of villages, exchanged compensation.

6

The Headman

MANY REFERENCES have been made to the headman and his place in village life: how he intervenes in quarrels, presides over the informal meetings of the elders, carries out sorcery, and so on. The office depends on popular esteem only, not on hereditary right, and we will now consider the method of his selection and appointment.

The native expression is *mwane-kama,* literally "man-big" (cf. *manu-kama,* meaning "bird-big," that is, the eagle). Sometimes the word is loosely applied to any hamlet senior, but, if pressed, the natives agree that at any given moment there is properly speaking only one real *mwane-kama* to a village. Usually he is easy to recognize. He is of mature years, over forty, at least; he carries himself with assurance and dignity; he lives in the most solidly built of the houses; he is outstandingly hospitable; on special occasions he may wear strings of shell discs below each knee and bracelets of porpoise teeth; and in former times, he would have had several wives. (Mbesa, the last Longgu headman of the old school, who died in 1920, was married to five, his immediate predecessor Tunggulu to over twenty.) The villagers also show him deference. If he joins a group those present wait for him to address them before speaking; they listen with attention to what he has to say; not unless he makes a jest do they introduce bawdy talk into the conversation; and although they, themselves, may clap one another on the back and slap one another playfully across the thighs, they take care to avoid physical contact with him.

The death of the headman of Mbambasu, a man named Monina, occurred during my stay in Longgu. Weeks after the funeral people were still expressing their regrets. During his lifetime, they said, the village had been "heavy" (*nggulua*); now that he was gone it would be "light" (*malamala*). The old excitements would be replaced by monotony, and there would be nobody to organize feasts or conduct dances. Yet, I had heard earlier many complaints about Monina's demands for assistance, which were held to be excessive, and it was even whispered in private that he was not averse to practicing *vele* sorcery against near neighbors whom he considered to be potential rivals.

The same ambivalence is apparent in the legendary tales of earlier headmen. The Longgu folk most often talk about Avi'a and Vonoa. These two reputedly enhanced the reputation of the place till it was talked about from end to end of Guadalcanal; but they also committed acts that are described with genuine horror. Avi'a ordered his followers to wipe out a visiting party of their trading partners, men whom they had a sacred duty to protect. While on the beach one evening, a mile or two from the settlement, he hailed a foreign vessel as it passed by and inquired where it was going. The crew failed to identify him in the gathering darkness and called out in reply, "To Longgu to see that old rogue Avi'a." Outraged at the insult, he that night gave instructions for the mass slaughter. Vonoa's behavior was even worse: he committed incest in public. His sister was in the cultivations helping him when the string of her grass skirt broke. As she stooped down to retrieve the garment he caught sight of her vulva and became inflamed with desire. He told the other workers to turn their backs, and he then threw the girl to the ground and had intercourse with her. It is stated that anyone else guilty of such an offense would have been speared on the spot by the women's close kinsfolk.

Despite this implication of power arbitrarily exercised, the headman's only strength lies in his influence over the villagers, as has been mentioned. At gatherings dealing with matters of policy, his job is to keep the proceedings orderly and, after deliberations are over, to voice the conclusions reached. Of course, his word carries weight, and he may be able to persuade waverers and those who are as yet uncommitted to support the line of action he advocates; but he can never impose his will against popular opinion. Indeed, a second set of legends or stories suggests that formerly headmen who consistently annoyed their supporters would have run the risk of being killed themselves. The approved method of killing a headman was for those who were disgruntled to inform the residents of some other settlement that the offending leader had repeatedly referred to them as his excrement. The warriors of that settlement would then steal upon the headman and cut off his head. Such a homicide did not call for vengeance.

Qualities Admired

To be considered suitable for headmanship a man must possess certain basic attributes. To win support, it is essential that he be forceful, even-tempered, tactful, industrious, a good speaker, and an able organizer. Previously there were also advantages in his enjoying renown as a warrior and magician. But the prime qualification is still wealth in the form of vegetable supplies and pigs.

Conditions in Guadalcanal are such that anyone who works hard can amass a fair surplus. A superabundance of foodstuffs, however, is of no direct benefit and can only be given away. Events of family importance—births, marriages, deaths, the construction of a new house or canoe, and so on—are celebrated with a feast. Each householder tries to provide as much as possible, and the one who continuously surpasses the rest in the lavishness of his hospitality and in the number of his guests builds up a great store of credits. The people are conscious of what they owe to him and express their sense of indebtedness by according him respect and added status. In other words, they acknowledge him as their headman.

Early Steps toward Status

Ambition becomes apparent in a man's early thirties, after he has settled down to the responsibilities of married life and is already surrounded by a young family. If he now entertains thoughts of raising his status, he begins cultivating larger gardens. His relatives are always ready to help, but when they do, as we have seen, he has to prepare a meal for them at the end of the day. At first a large number of workers would cause too heavy a drain on his resources, and he makes requests only to his closest kinsmen. Not until later are more and more assistants needed, and by then the food available exceeds the demand.

As his acreage of crops increases, so does the size of his pig herd. The man keeps the progeny of his own sows and begs one or two of the litter every time those of his kinsmen farrow. The task of feeding and tending the animals can be onerous, and to lighten the labor he may farm some of them out to his sisters and other relatives, with the offer of half the young piglets as a reward for the service.

After some time, when crop areas several acres in extent are flourishing and when there are perhaps ten fat pigs and several smaller ones in his sty, the man allows it to become known that he intends to erect a fine new dwelling, larger and better built and with a thicker thatch than is customary. This is tantamount to a public declaration that he is a candidate for the highest honors, though in practice many who begin with great plans find the drain on their energies so great that, after the house is completed, they abandon their hopes and resign themselves to a lesser role in the village life.

The work goes forward in the manner described earlier, except that more people take part, with a number coming from settlements farther afield. Correspondingly, the celebration to mark the end of the job, "The-feast-to-remove-the-splinters," as it is called, is considerably more elaborate. The following description relates to the feast of Atana, a villager already notable as a personage though as yet no rival to the acknowledged headman.

The house had been finished for a couple of weeks before preparations for the feast were begun. Atana, the men and youths of his hamlet, his other cousins, his brothers-in-law, and a selection of different relatives from other parts of the same clan then combined for a series of fishing expeditions. Each morning they paddled off in several canoes, and on returning in the evening, they smoked the catch on a frame erected over a long fire. At the end of ten days their baskets contained about 250 pounds of dried fish of various kinds. Meanwhile, Atana's wife, his sisters and sisters-in-law, and sundry other women relatives were collecting yams. They almost stripped his gardens and also took some from their own. The old dwelling, which had not yet been pulled down (though it was on the point of collapse), served as a storeroom, and eventually it contained over 5 tons of yams.

Atana now announced that the feast would take place in four days' time. His and his wife's working parties spent the first day collecting firewood and coconuts. The men brought in logs, the women bundles of sticks, and the youths strings of ripe nuts that they had picked off the ground. Next morning all worked together, chopping the logs and piling the pieces into tidy stacks alongside the ovens. Finally, on the third day, they occupied themselves making yam cakes. The women peeled a great quantity of tubers and grated the raw flesh while the men grated the meat of some of the coconuts and squeezed out the white cream. Both sexes now took banana leaves and wrapped up a series of sandwiches of layers of grated yam with cream in the middle. The 3000 or so of these sandwiches had to be cooked in a long row of earth ovens.

All this time individual households of persons less closely related to Atana had been making similar preparations. Each group caught a small amount of fish and baked a few packages of cakes.

At last the great day arrived. Everyone was up early and busy soon after sunrise. The women's main task consisted of making the remainder of the yams into puddings. They first carried the tubers to the stream for scraping and then set them in earth ovens to cook. Next, they began grating the rest of the coconuts and squeezing out the cream into great wooden bowls, in which it would be curdled with red-hot stones. By this time the yams were ready and could be taken out of the ovens. The women mashed them into a smooth paste with paddles, making quite certain that there were no lumps. In the final stage each pudding dish had alternate courses of paste and curdled cream. The un-colored, yellow, and purple yams had been kept separate so that in some dishes the mixture was white, in some pale gold, and in some pinkish-mauve.

While the women were occupied, the small boys went off to collect areca nuts and betel pepper. On their return the youths tied bunches of green nuts around the sides of each of the bowls and adorned the tops with orange-colored nuts, green pepper leaves, and white flowers.

All this while the men were attending to the pigs. They caught them with nets, tied their legs around a pole, strangled them with a stout rope, and singed off the bristles over a roaring fire; experts proceeded to carve the carcasses into joints. (It would be insulting to serve a guest pork that had been clumsily hacked up.)

By about three o'clock all the food stood in front of Atana's house. He and his immediate kinsmen had contributed the 250 pounds of dried fish, the 3000 yam cakes, 11 bowls of yam pudding, and 8 pigs.

Soon the Longgu villagers, together with some of the residents of the surrounding settlements, began drifting into the hamlet. Nearly everybody brought along some dried fish and a few yam cakes, and several of the leaders sent a pig and a bowl of pudding as well. On the final count the various heaps contained 300 pounds of fish, nearly 5000 yam cakes, 19 bowls of pudding, and 13 pigs.

The sexes kept apart, but men and women formed groups and sat at ease in the shade of the trees. A dozen or so youths, supervised by one of the elders, handed around areca nuts, betel pepper, tobacco, and green drinking coconuts.

Atana now made a count of all the people who had helped him—men, youths, women, girls. As he or a relative mentioned a name he placed a small pebble in a set of coconut shells, a procedure he checked twice to make certain that no one had been left out. (On some occasions I have seen the host make his way around the guests with a shell in his hand inviting each one to drop in the pebble himself; there were also times when, instead of using stones, he took a cord and tied a knot for every name.) Then he advanced to the center of the hamlet, followed by a crowd of helpers carrying armfuls of cakes. As he threw away the pebbles one by one, a helper placed two or three cakes on the ground. In the end these lay in long rows a couple of feet apart. Next, other men came along and placed more cakes, fish, and a joint of pork on top of the first cakes. When all the piles were complete Atana went around again, calling the names out loudly and indicating the heaps. This was the signal for the helpers to carry the food across to the individual concerned and lay it at his or her feet.

Now the leading men who had contributed a pig or a bowl of pudding were counted, and more piles were laid out for them. Each received a basket of fish, several cakes, a full leg of pork, and a bowl of pudding. In distributing these goods, Atana made sure not to give the same bowl back to the household from where it had come: to offer a person his own bowl would imply refusal to accept his gift.

Last of all, Atana's immediate relatives and those of his wife received extra portions. By that time he had made 257 separate presentations, and only the remnants were left as his share. People considered this proper. "The giver of the feast takes the bones and the stale cakes," runs the saying; "the meat and the fat go to others."

The villagers had looked forward to the festivities for days and talked of little else when they met to gossip during the evenings. The occasion was obviously a holiday, an opportunity for enjoyment and laughter. When the time for the festivity actually arrived, the younger folk put on their best clothing, and many wore valuable ornaments. The crowds remained in the hamlet till Atana had distributed the last morsel, and they watched all his moves with keen interest. The sight of the food gave great satisfaction, and whenever they had the chance those present handled the bowls and admired the decorations. The form of the garnishings called forth high praise, and such remarks as, "We shall eat till we sicken and vomit." They also told of earlier feasts and compared the amounts of food served. Sometimes, they said, the quantity was so enormous that much went bad and had to be thrown away. Whether overeating or lack of hygiene is responsible is not certain, but it is a fact that frequently an epidemic of gastroenteritis follows gatherings of this kind.

Further Advancement

If still anxious to advance himself, the householder must now consolidate his position by acquiring even more wealth. He has to cultivate larger gardens and breed extra pigs, not merely for his own use but to carry out exchanges with the Langalanga natives and others in order to build up stocks of shell discs and dog's and porpoise teeth.

Formerly it was at this stage that he began enlarging his household with additional wives. In later life he looked toward the attractions of youth, but at the start he usually preferred widows, who had better gardening experience than young girls. The spouse of a headman is obliged to work harder than other females, for, in addition to cultivating more gardens, she has to provide meals for the stream of visitors to whom her husband feels constrained to offer hospitality. The woman derives reflected prestige from her husband, however, and if she has a strong personality she achieves assured status in the community.

An individual whose status is rising is obliged to place his growing wealth at the disposal of close relatives and many others in the village. The feasts of ordinary folk are not as large as the one described, but everybody likes to make a good showing. They accept all contributions gladly, and the more the leader is forthcoming the greater is their admiration for him. He also helps with the presentations for the marriages of the youths who have served him well. But he does not only give: a small share of the bridal offerings to the girls of the hamlet generally goes to him.

Despite such generosity, the man must build up reserves so that, in due course, he can sponsor the series of entertainments connected with dancing. When he feels that he has enough reserves, the composition of a couple of new ballets to charm the spectators is an important consideration. He therefore confers with one of the few choreographers of the district, who may have to be sought in some village a dozen miles away or more. This person, if inspired to create something original, devotes himself to the job, picks out a few skilled local performers, and conducts rehearsals until each one knows his part. The prospective headman can then invite these and one or two additional men to be his principal dancers. Simultaneously, he engages another group to form the nucleus of the singers. (The natives of the interior of Guadalcanal have orchestras of panpipes, but on the coast the musical accompaniment for dancing is provided solely by a choir.)

When the preparations have reached this point the date is announced for the feast called "Bringing-the-dancers-to-central-area." The arrangements are similar to those for the house-building feast, except that more food is cooked and given away.

During the afternoon, when the puddings and joints of pork have been placed in neat rows, the leading dancers walk over to the middle of the hamlet. They form a column of fours, and any younger men who feel so inclined fall in behind. Behind these come the singers, with the youths and small boys right at the rear. Many of the performers are dressed up for the occasion with white cockatoo-feather headdresses, heavy necklaces or collars of shells and porpoise teeth, turtleshell earrings, shell breast plates, bead and rattan armbands, and fiber anklets stitched over with dried seed pods that clank with every movement. The dancers (but not the singers) carry a wicker shield and a spear.

The ballets are based on animal behavior or on everyday occupations—fishing, gardening, nutting—but so formal and conventionalized are the movements and gestures that rarely is it possible for an uninstructed observer to guess exacty what is being portrayed. The songs provide the rhythm, which is accentuated by the sound of the anklets, and all keep strict time. For some steps, the column advances and retires; for others the dancers turn into a single line. At first there may be confusion, especially in new ballets, as the leaders turn to left and right and wave their spears and stamp. But after practicing, the irregularities are straightened out and the company moves with the precision of guards on parade.

The average ballet takes from ten to fifteen minutes, and there is then a short pause. A full performance lasts about three hours, and the dancers then retire to wait for the food distribution.

During the next few months dances are held every week or two. The man responsible fixes the dates, but expects his principal performers to look after the details. On these occasions he provides each man with a meal, but there is no general feast.

As soon as perfection has been reached, the organizer arranges a "foreign" tour. He sends word to the headmen of a series of friendly villages that a visit will take place, and the party sets off. It spends a few days in each settlement and puts on a show every afternoon. The last evening before its departure from each village, the headman holds a feast in the party's honor and, as well as supplying the usual puddings and pork, rewards the chief dancers with a few strings of discs and the rest with dog's or porpoise teeth.

The senior men among the travelers, with profits in mind, bring along their prostitutes, but other females stay at home. Each day they are alone they hold a small dance of their own. Such women's dances are simple affairs without accompanying celebrations. The performers make a circle and go round and round with a slow shuffling tread. For music they have a chorus of older widows.

When the party returns the women welcome them with a dance, which is followed by a men's dance. This is the sole occasion when the sexes dance on the same day, and even then they do not perform together.

A second tour may follow after the lapse of a month or two, but at length, after perhaps a year, the dancing is brought to a close with the feast "Balm-for-the-aching-limbs." The biggest of these within living memory was given by the Longgu headman Mbesa, who himself supplied nearly fifty pigs and a colossal number of cakes and puddings. Other people gave twenty additional pigs and cakes in proportional amounts. At this last feast the dancers and singers must also be paid. The theory is that they have been working solely for the honor of the sponsor, though really, of course, they enjoy themselves thoroughly. The leaders receive sets of 10 or 12 strings, the members of the choir sets of about 8, and the rank and file sets of 4. Mbesa and his kinsmen in this way disposed of 350 strings. The presentation is always preceded by horseplay, in which the sponsor hurls pieces of fruit at each man before calling his name. The latter demonstrates his skill by protecting himself with his shield.

Dancing festivals are even more of a highlight than a feast alone. The rhythmical exercise is pleasant and invigorating, and those who take part, although they carry out the steps in unison, have excellent opportunities to gratify their vanity. Individual excellence is singled out for applause, and everyone is sure to win congratulations from somebody, even if only from a member of his family. Each person cherishes the hope that he will win recognition as an expert, for the name of such a person is remembered for years, especially if he is also a choreographer. But the spectators also are able to enjoy themselves. The ballets have great esthetic appeal and are often exciting.

Thus the community is further in the sponsor's debt, and he now assumes that he is well on the way to becoming a headman.

Yet there can be disappointments. Shortly before my first arrival in Longgu, the man Riani undertook a dance festival. His first feast was not lavish but still satisfactory, and practices for a tour were under way. Suddenly the seniors of the village began to have misgivings about his suitability for office. It was difficult to tell what had given rise to the doubts, but in discussing the matter with me a year afterwards they kept referring to Riani's overbearing manner and officiousness—qualities, so they said, that had previously never been noticed. Gradually the number of regular dancers dwindled until the tour had to be cancelled. For the final feast, contributions came from but one man outside the subclan—and he was a close patrilateral relative.

The Established Headman

Further progress requires a continuation of display to an even greater degree. There must be more and bigger housebuilding feasts, more and bigger dances. When the man's daughter has her face marked, he pays the operator a higher fee than another father would, and when his son marries he offers a larger bride price. He also builds a huge club for the men of the hamlet, furnishes a major share of the pigs when sacrifices are offered to the spirits concerned with the welfare of the village as a whole, and, when some leader has died, puts up the bulk of the wealth to reward the warriors who kill the sorcerer alleged to be responsible.

If he goes on doing all these things there is little doubt about his becoming the headman of his village. But, no matter how much food and other things he has given away, he can never rest on his laurels. As soon as his gardens begin to shrink in area and his herds cease to multiply, as well may happen when he becomes advanced in age and less active, he subsides into insignificance. There is always somebody just behind him in the race, waiting to pass should he falter or stumble.

Rival Headmen

The acknowledged headman is so accustomed to outgiving his fellow villagers that often he attempts the same tactics to outdo the headmen of the communities round about. He cannot exert any significant influence beyond the boundaries of his own settlement, except perhaps occasionaly through marriage alliances, but he may wish to secure enduring fame. So, if these other headmen provide 40 pigs for a feast he produces 60, and if they hold one dance festival he aims to give two.

One manifestation of this attitude is the competitive destruction of property, a custom known as *pinopolo,* which has affinities with the *potlatch* of the Haida and Kwakiutl Indians of North America.[1] In theory, the initiating headman takes precautions to avoid letting anyone know of his action, but if he were to do this seriously there would be no point in his behavior. Accordingly, he merely pretends to observe secrecy.

One morning Vatina, the headman of Longgu, asked his wife to hand over the baskets of valuables. He extracted several sets of discs, undid the calico wrappings, and threw the strings casually over one shoulder. Then he strode off toward the gardens, passing through the hamlet on his way under the gaze of a dozen or more of his relatives. Half an hour later he returned with his knees and arms covered with mud and clay. Somebody enquired where had he been, for as a rule people who have been gardening have a bath or a good wash before they re-enter the village. For a long time Vatina avoided answering and made all sorts of irrelevant remarks. Eventually, however, he agreed that he had buried the discs in the cultivations, though he protested that he would never have told us had we not so pestered him with our questions. Various of the men chided him, but he silenced them by reminding us that he was the headman and entitled to do as he liked with his own belongings.

The news soon spread, and while some clansmen scolded Vatina, other searched in vain for the right spot so that they could dig the discs up and hand them back. The rest of the villagers reacted in various ways. Many expressed pleasure at their association with a headman who could afford to be so wasteful, but there were a number who said cynically that it was all a put-up job and that later the strings would be surreptitiously extracted and find their way back to the baskets from which they had been removed.

Monina, the headman of Mbambasu, a couple of months later—and only

---

[1] See H. Codere, 1950.

six weeks before his death—did exactly the same kind of thing. As with Vatina, no one knew how many strings were buried, but from then on the Longgu villagers, including those who earlier had been so sceptical, boasted that certainly Vatina's must have been the greater number. This assertion they justified by pointing out the size of their settlement, which is bigger than Mbambasu, and by insisting that therefore it must be much the wealthier. The Mbambasu residents were not to be outdone. Their place might be smaller, they admitted, but it had bigger herds of pigs and more extensive gardens. Further, Monina was famous as far away as Malaita and Florida Islands, whereas Vatina was not even known on the far side of Guadalcanal.

7

Religion

GUADALCANAL RELIGION is founded on a belief in spirits possessed of a special power, *nanama,* that can be exerted for the benefit of the living. This has no ultimate source and is simply one of the regular attributes of supernatural beings, like their invisibility or ubiquity. Doubts are expressed about how exactly it works, and the general impression is that it is something akin to the power of the Christian God moving in a mysterious way His wonders to perform.

The natives maintain that their affairs would languish were *nanama* withheld. Its operation is revealed by results, and if a man's cultivations are prolific, if he catches plenty of fish, if his pigs multiply, or if he triumphs over his enemies, then obviously it must be working in his favor. People are agreed on the importance of skill and hard work and admit that an incompetent or lazy gardener will never reap a good harvest; but they insist that ultimately all success is the result of this benevolence of the spirits. So if of two men, both energetic, one prospers and the other fails, the reason is that the former has *nanama* behind him and the latter does not.

When talking about a neighbor who is making a reputation for himself, people are apt to remark that he "has" *nanama.* Similarly, in praising an example of clever workmanship, they may say that *"nanama* lies with the craftsman." These expressions are shorthand methods of speaking and in the literal sense are regarded as inaccurate. "The words are right, but the saying is wrong," one of my friends explained. "By himself a man is nothing, and we must all rely on what the spirits will do for us. *Nanama* has been twisted from the spirits to the person." The phrase "to have *nanama"* should therefore be taken as meaning "to flourish," but always with a rider understood—"as a result of forces from the other world."

Since *nanama* means so much, the people are always anxious to win the approval of the spirits. This they try to do by offering a sacrifice. Undue delay, they feel, angers the spirits and brings about suspension of *nanama,* an event necessarily leading to disaster.

The general term for spirit is *anggalo,* but three types are distinguished, and one of these is subdivided. There are the spirits of the dead, with those of outstanding warriors separated from the rest; spirits that may become incarnate as sharks; and spirits that can at will turn into snakes. Warrior, shark, and snake spirits are bound up with the wider social structure, and within a given locality the members of the same clan have a ritual relationship with an identical set of three, one of each kind. Such spirits are described as "great." The spirits of the ordinary dead, the "little" spirits, are concerned solely with individuals or, at most, with a subclan.

In the past the villages had shrines of the great spirits of all five of the clans, a total of fifteen, with an equivalent number of priests (*'aufia*) to take charge and superintend the sacrifices. Today, out of seventy-five shrines once scattered through Mbambasu, Longgu, Nangali, Mboli, and Paupau, only three survive, two in Mbambasu and one in Nangali. In addition, smaller shrines are located on the outskirts of the hamlets. Inside these last the residents preserve the skulls of their deceased forebears, women as well as men, but generally the handing over of an offering to their spirits does not need an official to act as an intermediary.

The word *pe'o* may be applied to any shrine, but often those of the great spirits are referred to as *ova ambu. Ova* is the term for a clubhouse, and *ambu* is the local version of the common Oceanic expression *tabu* or *tapu* (our word taboo is derived from it), meaning "sacred," "ritually unclean," "set apart," "forbidden."

The *nanama* of a warrior spirit brings victory in battle, that of a shark spirit security and good fortune at sea, and that of a snake spirit assured abundance in the gardens. In theory these benefits should accrue only to members of the clan, but in practice a spill-over occurs. When a settlement contemplated a raid, for instance, often the headman's sacrifice to the warrior spirit of his own group was held to be sufficient for the expedition, which was made up of men from all five of the units.

Nanama of ordinary spirits merely maintains the health of the living representatives of the hamlet. Sickness is accepted as a reminder of sacrifices too long delayed or forgotten, and when somebody is seriously ill and all magical remedies have proved unavailing, the patient and his near kinsmen think that perhaps it is time they paid their respects to the subclan ghosts.

Warrior Spirits

The warrior spirits of the villages with which we are here concerned are Ndave of Hambata clan, Unuasi of Lasi, Raunikaro of Naokama, Luvu of Thimbo, and Kulanikama of Thonggo. The first four are all said to have been noted during their lifetime for bloodthirstiness and the huge number of enemies they slew. Yet I could discover no details of their actual campaigns, and their deeds do not seem to be embedded in any legends. Curiously enough, the fifth, Kulanikama, is said to be the spirit of a woman. The story goes that she was making a pudding in her house at Nangali when suddenly the alarm sounded, indicating that the village was being attacked. Soon her husband was surrounded, and she sprang to his rescue with the only thing at hand, the paddle for mashing the yams. She brought this down on one of the fighters and crushed his skull. Then she rushed into the melee and slew several more. The rest, terrified to see this Amazon, fled in disorder.

Some of these spirits are worshiped in the Longgu area alone, but others are honored farther afield. In a village no more than 10 miles away, the Lasi and Thonggo spirits are respectively Irokavi and Sipolo instead of Unuasi and Kulanikama; on the other hand, Ndave is honored by all the Hambata clansmen throughout the full length of the coast, and Luvu by all the Thimbo clansmen for nearly the same distance. What happens is that in favorable circumstances the spirits of average individuals become elevated to the higher grade. If a subclan produces two mighty warriors in succession, the clan members throughout the village begin attributing the distinction of the second to the *nanama* of his predecessor. A mounting score of killings confirms their opinion, and now they, too, offer sacrifices to the same ghost. When, in time, a notable victory occurs, travelers on trading expeditions become impressed, and those of the right grouping may take the cult back to their own settlements.

Various seniors told me of earlier warrior spirits, now forgotten by other folk, whose names they had heard in childhood. Raunikaro and Luvu were comparative newcomers to Longgu, they maintained, and two generations ago the Naokama clansmen had looked to Sivosolo as their warrior spirit and the Thimbo clansmen to Putai. A couple of the oldest of my associates, one from Longgu, the other from Nangali, even put forward the view that the warrior spirits of the era of their great-great-grandfathers had not been the ghosts of humans. In that age, they said, each clan had as its war spirit a being that could turn itself into a crocodile. The probable explanation for the change was the introduction of guns, which were presented to the islanders in increasing quantities from about 1820 onwards, first by traders and later by the crews of vessels that came to carry off slaves for the plantations of Fiji, Samoa, and Queensland. Firearms altered the character of native warfare and sent the death roll soaring.

The two men made their statements in good faith, but although I am sure they genuinely believed what they said, I can hardly go beyond acknowledging the plausibility of the account. Crocodile spirits would have been fit companions for the shark and snake spirits and would also have possessed affinities with the eagle war spirits and the war spirits of poisonous serpents from the neighboring island of Malaita.[1]

Today, with fighting suppressed and Christianity becoming steadily more popular, only two warrior shrines remain, that of Kulanikama in Nangali and that of Unuasi in Mbambasu. Doubtless the reason for the survival of even

[1] See H. I. Hogbin, 1939, p. 108.

these is the tenacity of the ministering priests, who steadfastly refuse to relinquish their pagan religion.

Both shrines look from the outside like dwellings, except that thigh and other bones hang from the gable, and along the front a shelf supports a collection of skulls, many of them showing the mark of a blow from a club or hatchet. These are the trophies of former battles in which the *nanama* of the spirit whose house it is brought victory to the worshipers. The inside is bare, save for a mat where the priest occasionally sleeps and a pile of stones to be used in the oven for cooking the sacrifices. The only other item is a basket hanging from a hook attached to a rope tied to the ridge pole. In the one case the receptable holds a handful of shell discs said to have belonged to Kulanikama, in the other Unuasi's food bowl, together with portions of his sternum and skull.

The shrines that have disappeared are said to have been like these, except that those of Ndave and Luvu, spirits of men from distant villages, were without any relics.

Shrines are taboo, and, save when sacrifices are being presented, the priest alone enters them. At the same time, the villagers, women and men, make no attempt to avoid the vicinity, though I could never induce any of them, the Christian converts included, to handle the bones.

I had no opportunity to see a sacrifice, but the priest of Kulanikama, a man named Thaivo, related the procedures, and subsequently other men confirmed the account. First, there was formerly an annual ceremony connected with the ripening of the main Canarium-almond harvest. (This took place during December: there is a second but smaller harvest later.) All the men gathered a few nuts from their trees and brought them either to the house of the village headman or to that of the leading householder belonging to their clan. The headman or householder then carried the nuts to the priest, who got out his firesticks and kindled a new fire to burn them as an offering to the warrior spirit of the clan. (A householder wanting a fire would have tried to obtain glowing embers from a neighbor, but a priest was not allowed to take such an easy way out.) Afterwards everyone collected more nuts and was free to cook almond puddings as he pleased. Thaivo denied there was any notion that the great spirits were responsible for the yield of the almond trees. The people wished to share the bounty of the earth with the supernatural beings, he stated.

Then there were always sacrifices before a war party set off on a raid, or when the attack of an enemy force had been repulsed. These consisted of pigs, most of them supplied by the village headman. In the one case the priest asked the warrior spirit to exert its *nanama* to bring victory, in the other he expressed gratitude for its having done so. When the pigs had been caught and carried to the shrine he took one of them inside and trussed it up so that it hung several feet from the ground with its snout pointing upwards. There he let it remain until the next day. The men and women also brought vegetables and other foods from the gardens and made general preparations for a feast. In the early morning all the men assembled, and in their presence the priest dedicated the one pig to the spirit by rubbing it down with Cordyline and other leaves, which varied according to the spirit, and by calling out the spirit's name and also the names of the succession of earlier priests (eighteen for Kulani-kama). He then strangled the animal, cut it up, and removed the heart, which he cooked as the special share of the spirit, though he ate it himself. Subsequently assistants baked the meat and some of the vegetables in the oven within the shrine. This food was eaten solemnly by the males only, but the other pigs and the rest of the vegetables served as a general feast for everybody, including the youths and the girls. (The regulations about who might be present differed from spirit to spirit. For Luvu all children were forbidden.)

The only other occasion for sacrifices was when a leading man of the community was smitten with a disease that had failed to respond to magic and was threatening to become chronic. If a headman or some other person of standing had a long-continued attack of dysentery, for example, or a stubborn tropical ulcer, he thought that perhaps the warrior spirit of his clan had withdrawn *nanama* as a hint that it wanted a pig. Accordingly he had a young animal dedicated by the priest. He confined the pig in a sty so tiny that it could barely move and kept it stuffed with food until it grew monstrously fat. Then he handed it to the priest, who strangled it, cooked the heart, and distributed the pork. Sacrifices of this kind are still made to Kulanikama at Nangali and to Unuasi at Mbambasu.

The priest was in a state of taboo when he offered the sacrifices. He fasted from noon the previous day in preparation, and for the following two days he remained at the shrine and ate only food that he himself had baked. The stress was on avoiding all everyday affairs, not just those in which women were engaged, and on shunning meals cooked by anybody else, not merely those prepared by his wife and daughters. The absence of sexual discrimination in such matters was, for a Melanesian society, remarkable. I shall return to this point later.

The taboo also applied to the male members of the congregation during a sacrifice, though to a lesser extent. They fasted for the morning of the ceremony; they refrained from gardening, fishing, and other work during the following evening only. If they wanted anything to eat, apart from their share of the sacrificial pork, they had to cook it themselves, and before actually consuming it, perform a small ceremony called *toitava*. This consisted of entering one of the clubs and there touching a package believed to contain an areca nut that had been dedicated to the spirits. (The priest, it is to be noted, was not obliged to carry out *toitava*.)

Taboos of this kind were most onerous during the period when a shrine was rebuilt. Before the job could start, a small hut had to be erected alongside, and to this the priest translated the relics of the dead warrior, the oven stones, and the war trophies. The men then tore down the old structure and burned it before starting on the new work. They toiled as fast as possible without taking any days off for other tasks. Thus the new place was soon ready, and everything could be quickly returned. Half a day's fast preceded the undertaking; while it was in progress, and it always lasted several days, the workers col-lected and cooked their own food, performed the *toitava* ceremony before eating, and refrained from chewing betel nut and from smoking. Yet they could sleep with their wives in the family dwelling.

In olden days each corner post of the renovated shrine had to be planted on a dead body to ensure that there would be a spirit to hold the timber firm against tempests. Nobody now living had seen this done, and I could obtain no further information beyond the fact that the corpses were secured from hostile villages in the interior.[2]

Surprisingly, although spirit and clan are so firmly linked, the priest was free to choose, within certain limits, who should succeed him. He could trans-mit his knowledge of the ritual to his brothers, his sons, and his uterine nephews. Then, when the time came, he picked out the one who satisfied him best. More often than not, to judge from genealogies (admittedly inadequate for the early generations), he seems to have favored a son, who necessarily be-longed to a different clan from his own. There was a pronounced feeling, never-theless, that after a lapse the office ought to go back to the group. With this in mind, Thaivo, who is himself of Lasi clan, had seen to it that both his sons were married to girls of Thonggo clan, the unit from which Kulanikama had come. (Subsequently, to his great regret, both men embraced Christianity.)

Thaivo also discussed with me the spread of a cult. If a headman from some outside village wished to establish the worship of Kulanikama in his own community, a request would come for relics, oven stones, and ashes from the shrine. Whether or not some of the bone fragments or discs were handed over depended on what was still available. No objection would be raised, however, to the oven stones or ashes. The visitor first offered a pig to Kulanikama, and after it had been eaten the priest took four of the stones and four handfuls of ashes to serve as a nucleus for the new shrine. In addition, someone from the other settlement, who was necessarily of the right clan, had to learn the ritual for the sacrifices, including the special leaves to be used and the names to be recited. Later the cult might be passed on in exactly the same way from this community to others with which it had friendly relations, settlements not neces-sarily visited by the people of Nangali or Longgu.

Shark Spirits

These are Vaurangga of Hambata, Pota of Lasi, Loiloi of Naokama, Mbesavu of Thimbo, and Saubaina of Thonggo. No others are known, and the same five are worshiped all the way along the coast as far as the clans persist. Again a full-scale mythology is lacking, though individuals tell stories of how the shark spirit of the clan intervened to save a forebear from certain death. Thus Avi'a relates that when his grandfather's canoe had a hole torn in the bot-tom by striking submerged wreckage half way across the strait between Guadal-

---

[2] C. E. Fox, 1962, records a similar custom from San Cristoval.

canal and Malaita, the spirit of the Thimbo clan, whose priest he was, transformed itself into a shark and blocked the hole with its dorsal fin so that the crew could paddle the vessel to the shore. Vatina's maternal uncle, too, was saved from death by a similar visitation. The man's canoe had foundered in a gale, throwing those on board into tempestuous seas. The wild sharks circled round, but the spirit shark appeared and drove them away, allowing the party to swim to an island nearby, from which they were later rescued.

Every one of the shark priests from the Longgu area is now a Christian, and although the sites of the shines are still pointed out, they are overgrown with weeds. They were never houses, just clear spaces with clumps of red croton bushes and other plants, which are for some reason associated with the other world, surrounding a pile of oven stones.

Regular sacrifices took place at the opening of each bonito season. Every priest sent out a canoe when the first shoal appeared after the change in weather, and later he threw part of the entrails of one of the fish into the sea and burned the rest on a fire near the sacred oven. Other people were now free to go fishing whenever they cared to do so.

Then there were the occasional sacrifices, of which the most important were those preceding the dispatch of a fleet of trading canoes. As usual, the village headman supplied the biggest share of the pigs. The ritual was similar to that accompanying the sacrifices to the warrior spirits, except that the priest, instead of roasting the heart, threw it into the sea. After eating the pork, the worshipers "showed themselves to the shark" by walking into the water until they could no longer stand up. From time to time the village leaders also offered a pig or two for the purpose of ensuring the continuance of *nanama* in the day-to-day fishing expeditions, and they always sacrificed several pigs after an earthquake to prevent further destruction. Nobody could explain the connection between the shark spirits and seismic disturbances, but the reason may well have been the disastrous tidal waves that occasionally drove far inland, causing much loss of life and damage to property. Finally, there were sacrifices associated with persistent ill health. The diseases, unlike those for which the warrior spirits were responsible, were all related to the respiratory system, when the patient, as in a case of asthma, had trouble breathing "as though he were drowning."

The taboos were of the familiar kind, but with two additions. Consumption of bonito was absolutely forbidden on the same day a person had eaten bananas or pork, and while in a canoe he had to avoid fruit and meat. At such times the diet consisted of vegetables or nuts.

Snake Spirits

These are all female, probably because gardening is primarily the concern of the women. The reptiles into which the spirits can transform themselves are of the python species. Far from harming people, they are a help in that they live on rats, which eat the seed yams. A python in the thatch of a storehouse is the best omen possible.

The term for the snake spirits, *vi'ona,* is a dialectal variation of the San Cristoval *hi'ona* or *figona,* and it is from this island that they are supposed to have come. (The San Cristoval cults are dealt with at length by C. E. Fox, 1924, Chap. 6.) The information about them, as with the other great spirits, is fragmentary. The account of the snake spirit Watumbale of Lasi clan, for example, relates that in San Cristoval it had a human daughter, who married and gave birth to an infant. When she went to the gardens, the mother was in the habit of leaving the child in the care of its snake grandmother. One day the husband reached home first and became alarmed at the sight of the baby in the coils of a serpent, which he did not know was really a spirit. He took a stick to kill it, but it escaped into the sea and swam to the north coast of Guadalcanal. Here it wandered about from water hole to water hole in search of a home, until eventually it came to Moli village in the southeastern corner, where it finally settled. The different villages built shrines along the places where it had stopped, and it was at these shrines that the sacrificial pigs were presented. Today nearly all the snake priests are Christians, and but one shrine remains, that of Watumbale at Mbambasu. Regular offerings were made at the opening of the main yam harvest, occasional offerings when the headman Monina, who was of Lasi clan, had a feast in mind and wished to be ready with extra supplies.

Clan Spirits and the Village

In a previous section I mentioned that, despite the statements that a great spirit devotes its *nanama* solely to the members of its own clan, in practice a sacrifice is accepted as beneficial to the community at large. Usually the headman takes over the responsibility for organizing the ceremony and supplying most of the pigs, and it is to the great spirits of his clan, therefore, that the main offerings are made. The upshot is that during his lifetime these three spirits come to assume greater significance than those of the remaining clans. The present Longgu headman, Vatina, a pagan till his recent conversion, belongs to Thimbo clan, and what are properly Thimbo great spirits have almost come to be looked upon as village deities. In Nangali, their place is taken by the spirits of the Thonggo headman's clan and in Mbambasu by those of the Lasi headman's clan. A switch occurs when the old leader dies, and the spirits of his group are replaced by those of the successor's unit.

Funeral Ritual

The beliefs and practices concerned with the spirits of ordinary men and women cannot be understood without some knowledge of the mortuary ceremonies.

Usually all the close relatives are at hand when anyone dies, but if not, they are sent for at once. The person bearing the message, should he be of the same clan as the deceased, is permitted to say that the man or woman is dead (*mae*), but should he belong to another clan he employs a euphemism and speaks of him or her as being bad (*ta'a*). Most of the people smash some minor item as an expression of grief, but the chief heirs destroy not only a part of their present property but also a portion of what they are about to inherit. On several occasions I saw them drive an ax through the bottom of a canoe and chop down fruit trees and coconut palms. (When felling palms they always pick out an even number lest "death should strike again to complete the pair.") Widowers behave in similar fashion when a wife has died.

The corpse is prepared by women from clans other than that of the deceased, though they must not be the actual sisters-in-law or daughters-in-law. They wash the body, adjust the facial muscles and the hair, dress it in new garments, and arrange it in the center of the house so that it is shown to the best advantage. Various immediate male kinsfolk, such as the father, husband, sons, maternal uncles, and uterine nephews then lay valuables, including strings of discs and collars of teeth, on the mats alongside the body.

While these tasks are being carried out, the mother, wife, daughters, maternal aunts, and uterine nieces sit weeping in the background. Now they advance and lie down beside the body, wailing loudly as if in an abandonment of despair. Doubtless some of them are indeed miserable, but convention obliges them to give a public demonstration, regardless of their personal feelings.

By this time the other villagers have begun to assemble. The women enter for a few minutes in small clusters and weep aloud, but the majority of the men seat themselves outside and remain silent. As the parties arrive on the scene, one or another of the men of the hamlet or a close relative living elsewhere steps forward and presents each person with a dog's tooth or a few porpoise teeth "in payment for the tears."

Meanwhile, the women of the dead person's subclan, together with those married to the men of the subclan, have started seeing to a meal. They take yams both from the gardens of the deceased and from their own, scrape them, and place them in the oven. When the visitors have sat for an hour or two, they also think about eating. The women go home and cook, and the men collect green coconuts for drinking and areca nuts and betel pepper. They all return to the place of mourning late in the afternoon, carrying dishes. Some of the chief mourners now make a distribution. The members of the bereaved family eat nothing, but the rest partake of the food.

That night all the people of the village and many of the residents of the surrounding settlements stay close by. They sit chatting in groups around small fires, many of them with sleeping children in their arms. Etiquette demands their presence but does not insist that they should wear long faces or pretend to be grief-stricken. After they have said all that they can think of on the subject of their loss, they turn to other topics. Gradually, one by one, they fall asleep. In the morning they drift away without formally announcing their departure to the mourners inside the house.

As dawn breaks, the eldest sister's son of the deceased, or some relative of the same subclan acting for him should he be still a child, breaks a green coconut and allows the liquid to fall on the corpse. The last mortal remnants are thus washed away. Then, if the dead person is a male, the senior member of the subclan prays to the spirit for the first time and asks it to exercise its *nanama* to the advantage of both the subclan and the subclan of the children. He also pulls out a handful of hair from the corpse, wraps it in a small mat, and sends it to the clubhouse to be placed on a high shelf. It is supposed to be a receptacle for the *nanama* and thus brings good fortune to all who enter the building. Everything is now ready for the disposal of the body.

The commonest method of dealing with the dead is burial beneath the floor of the dwelling, but corpses may be buried outside, sealed in a cage of cane and palm leaf, taken out to sea, or exposed on a rock. The choice depends on such factors as the traditions of the subclan, the wishes of the deceased, and the convenience of the survivors. Shark priests, however, are invariably buried in the sea.

If burial under the house is decided upon, there is still the question of whether the body should be placed in an extended or in crouched position. The relatives choose the position and then take a collection of new mats as coverings. They wrap up the body, leaving with it the valuables that were placed alongside. Two of the affines dig a shallow grave, but before covering it they pass a long bamboo through the thatch so that the end of the tube rests on top of the corpse's head.

The widow or widower, the bereaved parents, the sons and daughters, and the sisters' sons and daughters are in a state of taboo for the period of mourning, which lasts two or three months. They mostly stay in the house, but may not have a fire and still less cook there; they are also forbidden to wash or shave. During this time they depend upon kinsfolk to bring them raw food, which each of them cooks for himself at the side of the dwelling. Their sole duty is to spend a couple of hours or so each day pouring water down the bamboo tube to keep the head of the corpse moist, thereby ensuring rapid decomposition of the flesh.

The senior man of the subclan, because he pulled out the hair, and the gravediggers are also taboo, but for ten days only. They remain secluded in the club and cook their own food, carefully performing the purifying ceremony of touching the areca-nut bundle (*toitava*) before each meal.

For the rest of the people who visited the house of death, a sprinkling of coconut fluid suffices to remove the contamination.

Persons of no social consequence are buried outside the house. They include elderly men and women who die without leaving a surviving heir and also young children. Those who touch such corpses are still taboo, but there are no true mourners who seclude themselves for a couple of months as with other deaths.

Affines construct the receptable if the cage method of burial is adopted. The bamboo is adjusted to reach the top of the head, and the mourners pour water down each day. Affines also carry the body if the relatives decide to expose it on a rock. Decomposition is then so rapid that the water is unnecessary.

For burial at sea the affines first tie sealed baskets of stones either to the waist or the feet of the body, according to whether the person has expressed a wish "to sit down" or "to stand up" in the water. On each occasion that I attended three canoes took part, the first bearing the affines and the corpse, the second the immediate male kinsfolk, and the third interested male relatives from more distant localities. The canoe for the corpse was already afloat before the body was placed on board, a precaution to ensure its being kept dry until the total immersion. The fleet went beyond the reef, about half a mile from the shore, and the body was then gently lowered into the water. On one occasion a son of the deceased dived down with it "because of affection," but his action was unusual. Afterwards, each canoe made four rapid circles—why I could not discover—and immediately the crews caused the craft to capsize, throwing everybody into the sea. The wetting removed the defilement of death. Had it been omitted, the canoes would subsequently have been useless for fishing.

Throughout the weeks of mourning the villagers refrain from making unnecessary noise, partly out of respect, partly lest they should be suspected of rejoicing at the death and as a result be accused of performing sorcery. They do not shout or sing, they postpone building new houses, and, if obliged to clear land for gardens, choose plots so far away that the sound of the ax strokes will not be heard in the settlement. At last the day comes—whether the body has been buried under the dwelling, placed in a cage, or exposed—when the flesh is so decayed that the skull can be removed. For this operation the chief heir engages an expert who has a knowledge of the appropriate protective magic. The man sends everybody away and proceeds to take up the head and clean it. When ready, he hangs it under the eaves in the front of the house. The heirs now return and present him with quantities of valuables for his trouble. He is, of course, taboo, and in consequence compelled to retire to the club.

During the next few days, certain outstanding payments are made. If a woman has died, the widower hands over a few strings of discs to her brothers in case they may be thinking he neglected her; if a man has died the widow acquires discs from her brothers and gives them to her husband's brothers; if a child has died the father presents discs to his wife's brothers. Shortly afterwards the recipients return the compliment with a larger amount, thereby showing their gratitude for the due performance of the mortuary rituals. At this point the widow offers her husband's garments, which hitherto she has worn around her neck. The brother or nephew of the deceased accepts the clothing and burns it.

The feast to terminate the mourning follows. For this the carcasses of wild pigs and vegetables and fruits that grow wild in the forest have to be collected. The subclansmen of the dead person and a few other close relatives supply the food, which they present uncooked to the rest of the villagers. Next day the senior man of the subclan places the skull in the hamlet shrine and sacrifices a small pig in front of the shrine to the spirit. The cycle is now complete, and things return to normal.

The Remains of the Dead

Each of the minor shrines includes two repositories, one for the skulls of the males, the other for those of the females. More commonly they take the form of a small cist constructed of large flat stones, but a few are thatched sheds raised up 3 or 4 feet on piles. They contain nothing but the heads, which are so placed that they all face the sea. Cordyline, croton, and other colored shrubs grow close by, and, at a distance of 5 yards or so, is a solid fence or a wall of coral boulders. In one example, at Nangali, the posts of the palisade are carved and painted with native pigments to represent human figures, weapons, birds, and fish.

When asked, people reply that a person's skull must rest in the shrine of the subclan to which he or she belonged: in practice, many sons request the skull of the father, out of filial affection, for their shrine; and many a husband wants his own and his wife's skulls to rest near each other. The clansmen never refuse permission.

In the past the shrines were periodically cleaned and repaired, and on such occasions those who took part were under a taboo. The adult men of the hamlet did the actual work, but while the job was in progress the youths held the skulls on their knees. Accordingly, the boys were subject to the more severe restrictions. The men withdrew to the club and cooked their own meals—always touching the areca nut bundle before eating—for a mere couple of days; the youths were set apart for a month. One of the seniors took charge of them and made sure that they kept out of sight, stole all their food from the gardens and cooked it themselves, and refrained from bathing. At the end he told them to steal a pig, which they cooked and ate before returning to their families.

Worship of the Dead

The natives refer to a person's shadow and his reflection in a mirror or a forest pool by the same term, *nunu*. At death, but not before, so they say, both become spirits, respectively the *anggalo* and the *anoa*. The former possesses *nanama* and remains around the village, whereas the latter, like the Christian soul, passes to another world (located on the rocky island of Marapa off the eastern end of Guadalcanal) and takes no further interest in human concerns. *Anggalo* of the dead, normally invisible, may show themselves as fireflies, which are greatly feared. One evening a neighbor came running to my house asking for kerosene in which to bathe his face because a firefly had alighted on his cheek.

Just as the fiction is current that village residents dance solely to please their headman, so it is maintained that mourners perform mortuary rites for the satisfaction of the deceased. People state that if a leader showers gifts on the men who come to do him honor, then surely the spirit ought to reward those who put up with the inconvenience of seclusion and the discomfort of tending the grave. They say that in such circumstances the expectation of *nanama* is reasonable and proper. It follows that a householder has no thought of making a sacrifice until compelled to do so by magic-resistant disease. Persistent illness he accepts as the indication that the spirit has withdrawn its *nanama* because it insists on an offering. He has a kinsman seek out a brush turkey's egg, which he requests the head of the subclan to burn at the shrine; or he dedicates a young pig for presentation later, after it has been fattened. Again the subclan leader acts as master of ceremonies and treats the pig's heart, but all the men of the group receive a share of the pork.

Most people believe that a spirit makes demands on the subclan members alone. So, normally a brother sacrifices for a sister and a maternal uncle for a youthful uterine nephew or niece. But occasionally a dutiful husband takes over the responsibility for a wife and a fond father for a young son or daughter.

Women's Taboos

Generally in Melanesia, the social differences between the sexes are reinforced by the requirements of the religious system. In the majority of the societies men are held to be sacred while in the act of carrying out the most manly of the occupations. Participants in important ceremonies, workers engaged in major economic undertakings, and warriors during the course of a campaign are all engaged in such activities and are therefore forbidden, on pain of supernatural punishment, to have any contact with females. Correspondingly, while pursuing purely female activities, women are regarded as ritually unclean. After giving birth to a child and when menstruating they also are set apart and must avoid the company of males. Sometimes a single word covers the concepts of both "sacred" and "ritually unclean"; sometimes there are distinct terms.

We have observed that Guadalcanal is exceptional in that men when taboo (*ambu*) are cut off from everybody, male as well as female. Guadalcanal women are even more unusual. The taboo of childbirth (*ambu*) demands that they also retire completely; but they are not subjected to any restrictions whatsoever during menstruation. I can offer no explanation for the anomaly, but am convinced that it is unconnected with matrilineal descent. Females have the same social status here as elsewhere, and the barriers against them are just as formidable.

Children are expected to begin life on the territory of their clan, and toward the end of a woman's pregnancy the sisters erect a small hut for her on the outskirts of the brothers' hamlet in the part of the bush that serves the female residents as a latrine. The husband and brothers also engage a midwife, whom they choose partly for her experience, but mainly on account of her advanced age; she must be so ancient, so close to death, that the contaminating blood of childbirth can scarcely do her any harm. She and the expectant mother retire to the shed as soon as the labor pains begin, and it is here that the child is born. The mother, mother-in-law, sisters, and sisters-in-law wait nearby, ready to bring hot water and anything else needed, but they leave their burdens outside and on no account touch the woman or even look at her. In olden days the first-born was taboo and had always to be killed. The midwife put it outside for the maternal uncle to deal with, and as a rule he strangled it and threw it into a hole in the forest. Subsequent infants, however, were tenderly cared for.[3]

Three days after the birth the woman's husband and brothers collaborate in the construction of a better hut closer to the houses of the hamlet, and to this the nurse conducts her charge after night has fallen. For the next ten days the sisters and husband's sisters bring vegetable broth for the woman and solid food for the midwife, but they still put the bowls down outside the door.

On the morning of the fifteenth day after delivery, mother and midwife take a ritual bath and rub themselves with scented herbs, over which the older woman has murmured a charm. They are now free to return to the village, and the baby can be given a name. On the next fine morning, the mother, accompanied by the father, carries the child to the cultivations "to show it to the yams." Later the father pays the midwife with a large supply of food, including either a wild pig or a basket of dried fish. The mother's brothers are not obliged to help him, but always do so. The old woman derives prestige from sharing the goods among her kinsfolk.

The father and mother observe various food restrictions for a period of about a year until the baby can walk. These are magical in intention and not at at all associated with the birth taboo. They refrain from eating pork lest the child should have fits, from eating certain fish lest it should have bulging eyes, and from turtle meat lest it should develop a horny skin.

A menstruating woman wears skirts of dark banana leaf, not as a distinguishing mark but because these, being easy to make, are readily expendable. If suffering no discomfort, she goes about her work in a normal manner, minding the children, gardening, and cooking the meals. It is doubtful whether the husband would be willing to cohabit with her, but his avoidance is based on esthetic considerations, not on religious belief. Unless he is the priest of a great spirit, however, he has no hesitation about eating food that she has handled.

Magic

Sacrifices are aimed at securing the benefits of *nanama* for human affairs in general or for the success of important enterprises. Yet the offerings are by themselves insufficient, and the natives also perform magic to pin the *nanama* down to the details of everything that is dangerous or of which the outcome is uncertain. In warfare there is magic to inspire the warriors with bravery, to enable them to creep up on the enemy unobserved, to cause the weapons to inflict lethal wounds, and to make the enemy sluggish and weak; in overseas trading

---

[3] The custom of killing the first-born has also been reported from San Cristoval. See C. E. Fox, 1962, p. 144: "The first-born baby was always killed. The father took it to the beach, dug a little hole, put the baby in with a large stone on top, and stamped on the stone."

to give the canoes eyes to see the correct destination, to prevent squalls, to calm the wind, to confer such beauty on each member of the party that his partner will present him with a great quantity of goods; in fishing to bring a great haul; and in gardening to preserve the fences, to drive away plant diseases and insects, to bring the sun or the rain, and to make the yams increase in size. Other rites are performed to cause disease, to cure it, to accelerate delivery when a woman is in labor, to attract a lover, to multiply the pig herd, to prevent a nut collector from falling when he climbs a high tree, and to ensure that the amount of food provided for a feast will satisfy all the guests.

The term for magic is *aru,* which is actually the word for the spell; but each different kind of magic has a name of its own. Magic aimed at bringing misfortune to an enemy—disease, death, or the destruction of property—is *kimbo;* war magic, *nggoni-mala'ai;* fishing magic, *nggoni-i'ia;* garden magic, *susu;* health magic, *nggoni-nggoni;* weather magic, *nggoni-thalu;* and so on. (*Nggoni* means to arrange, to prepare; *nggoni vau,* to arrange the mats for sleeping; *nggoni uvi,* to arrange the yams in a basket ready for carrying; *nggoni-i'ia,* to arrange the fish; and *nggoni-thalu,* to arrange the clouds.)

Magic belongs to all time and is eternal. Much of it goes back to the giants who first inhabited the world. These beings regularly used it and either handed it over to the earliest men, or else the primeval ancestors stole it from them. Other forms came from the great culture heroine Koevasi, and still others were obtained from foreigners who sold their knowledge for a price to trading partners. The secrets form a valued part of a man's property, and he teaches them to those who will come after him.

Almost all magic has three elements: the spell, the vehicle through which the spell works, and the rite. The verbal formula of the spell is always rhythmical to facilitate learning and subsequent recall, and, as absolute accuracy in repetition is considered essential, it often abounds in archaisms; sometimes, indeed, the meaning of particular expressions has been lost. The first, and longer section states over and over again that the desired end has already been achieved. This part is rich in similes, metaphors, and other figures of speech. It is followed by a request to the former owners of the magic to exert their *nanama.* The following is an example of fishing magic.

> My pearl-shell hook is shining brightly.
> It shines like the sun in the early morning across the sand,
> Like the full moon striking the white of the reef,
> Like phosphorescence dripping from the end of my paddles,
> Like red flowers in the darkness of the forest.
> My pearl-shell hook goes down into the water.
> The fish from far away, from Aola and from Marau,
> They see it and swim to look.
> They struggle to enjoy it, fight one another to take it.
> I pull them up—one, two, three, four, five—
> So large nobody has seen their equal.
> *Nanama* Riani, *nanama* Inonisondo,
> Tilani, Totovele, Sutu, Selo, Kikithia, Kuki,

Sasaka, Seka, Vonoa, Vuria, Kavora, Kapini,
Upolu, Ulua, Ngangenda, Ndambonoa, Tete, Vavasi,
Nanama, nanama, nanama.

The second element, the vehicle, usually referred to as *ria,* "ginger," a common ingredient, consists of a bundle of objects, generally of vegetable origin, chosen because of some real or fancied resemblance to the objective. The vehicle of the spell just quoted is made up of four vividly-colored flowers and leaves; in beauty magic it consists of sweet-scented herbs; in gardening magic of the bark of several of the largest trees; in rain magic of the skin of melons and other juicy fruits.

To understand the rite it is necessary to know that a Guadalcanal native thinks the heart is both the core of life and the seat of the intellect. A person learns a magical system, and the knowledge lodges with his breath in the throbs beneath his ribs. When he recites a spell he has therefore to breathe hard on the vehicle and at the end of each line of the verse drench it with a fine spray of saliva. By this means the bundle of leaves or other objects becomes charged with vital force. The man places it in contact with whatever is to be influenced and is content to believe that he will now achieve what he wants. Sometimes, in addition, he is called upon to go through a pantomime. In magic for fishing, for instance, he makes the motions of hauling in a big catch; in magic to overcome fear he assumes a menacing attitude; in magic for beauty he pretends to stroke soft smooth flesh; and in that to cause sore feet, he limps.

The Christians apply the word *aru* to their prayers. They explain that prayer and spell are similar in action, except that the one is directed toward God and the other toward the ancestors. The pagans nevertheless behave as though magic can be depended upon implicitly—provided, that is, there are no mistakes in either the spell or the rite. They say that a petition made up on the spur of the moment is less effective because the expressions were not employed by the persons whose spirits are being addressed. This statement implies that the random plea lacks the authority of tradition. The spell is sanctioned by long usage, and the list of names is proof of its potency for the present owner. Had these men found it unavailing they would never have continued to pass it down through the generations. At the same time, people deny that magic achieves its end directly. It coerces the spirits to do the work through their *nanama.* "*Nanama* comes out from my heart with the breath as I say the words," one man told me. Magic is thus regarded as something possessed by men that enables them to direct the forces of the supernatural world for their own ends.

One irregular type of agricultural magic demands special consideration in that it lacks a spell. Several men own smooth rounded stones that have a superficial resemblance to a yam. These are supposed to be petrified sections of a snake spirit, or to have been in contact with a snake spirit. People say that it is necessary only to place the stones in the garden, together with some special leaves, to produce a bumper crop. My friend Hali had such a stone, which his grandfather had obtained from a snake priest in the Marau district. The priest took it from a water hole where the snake spirit had once lived and passed it to the grandfather with instructions to place it in the middle of each cultivation after planting at the four corners the leaves of the *aikambo* tree (it has very large fruit), the *lami* tree (it has smooth bark), the *ainiola* tree (it has luxuriant foliage), and the *alori* tree (it is so hardy as to be almost indestructible). "My yams," said Hali, who is a Christian, "are still like the *aikambo,* the *lami,* the *ainiola,* and the *alori.*"

Nanama and *Mana*

The concept of *nanama* in some ways resembles that of "luck," except that normally we do not connect luck with supernatural beings. Because science enables us to direct our operations better and reduce the element of chance, luck also has narrower application for us. Yet many Europeans still carry out such magical acts as consulting the stars, knocking on wood, and scattering salt in an endeavor to bring luck under control.

The word *nanama* is a linguistic variant of the expression *mana,* which is widespread (but by no means universal) in the Pacific islands. It was first mentioned by the missionary Codrington in an early book about the Melanesians, with whom he worked.[4] His study has given rise to such a great deal of theorizing that we might at this point benefit by considering his account.[5]

Codrington summed up the notion of *mana* as follows.

There is a belief in a force altogether distinct from physical power, which acts in all kinds of ways for good and evil, and which it is of the greatest advantage to possess or control. This is *Mana.* . . . It is a power or influence, not physical, and in a way supernatural; but it shows itself in physical force, or in any kind of power or excellence which a man possesses.

The Melanesian's mind is entirely possessed by the belief in a supernatural power or influence, called almost universally *Mana.* This is what works to effect everything which is beyond the ordinary power of men, outside the common processes of nature; it is present in the atmosphere of life, attaches itself to persons and to things, and is manifested by results which can only be ascribed to its operation.

So far my conclusions are in agreement, though I would hesitate to subscribe to the statement that *mana* "is present in the atmosphere of life" because I do not understand what is meant by this.

---

[4] R. H. Codrington, 1891, pp. 118 to 120.

[5] R. Firth, 1940, pp. 483 to 512, criticized several of the theories at some length. To illustrate how curious some of them were, I quote the following, in translation, from H. Hubert and M. Mauss, 1904, pp. 109 to 112: "The idea of *mana* is one of those confused notions that we believe we ourselves have got rid of and which, in consequence, we find difficulty in understanding. It is obscure, vague, and yet in its use strangely definite. It is abstract and general yet full of the concrete. Its primitive nature, that is to say, complex and obscure, forbids us making a logical analysis: we have to be satisfied with a description. . . . The idea of *mana* consists of a number of unstable concepts that merge into one another. It is by turns and simultaneously quality, substance, and activity. . . . It is also a kind of ether, imponderable, communicable, which spreads by itself."

He went on in words almost identical with my own.

If a man has been successful in fighting, it has not been his natural strength of aim, quickness of eye, or readiness of resource that has won success; he has certainly got the *mana* of a spirit or of some deceased warrior to empower him, conveyed in an amulet of stone around his neck, or a tuft of leaves in his belt, in a tooth hung from the finger of his bow hand, or in a form of words with which he brings supernatural assistance to his side. If a man's pigs multiply, and his gardens are productive, it is not because he is industrious and looks after his property, but because of the stones full of *mana* for pigs and yams that he possesses. Of course, a yam naturally grows when planted, that is well known, but it will not be very large unless *mana* comes into play; a canoe will not be swift unless *mana* be brought to bear upon it, a net will not catch many fish, nor an arrow inflict a mortal wound.

This *mana* is not fixed in anything and can be conveyed in almost anything; but spirits, whether disembodied souls or supernatural beings, have it and can impart it, though it may act through the medium of water, a stone, or a bone. All Melanesian religion consists, in fact, in getting this *mana* for one's self, or getting it used for one's benefit—all religion, that is, as far as religious practices go, prayers and sacrifices.

The only exception that could be taken to this statement is that the assertions "*mana* can be conveyed in almost anything" and "it acts through the medium of water, a stone, or a bone" are insufficiently precise. Each system of magic has its own substances for the conveyance of *mana,* and a stone, for instance, is adequate only if it is traditionally associated with the system in question. If croton leaves, let us say, are called for, then a stone is useless.

The limitation of Codrington's account arises rather from what he left out. Nowhere did he distinguish clearly between *mana* and magic, and as a result a number of the theoretical writings sought the origin of magic in *mana.*[6] I stress again that *mana* is a supernatural force, and, despite occasional linguistic usage, it never resides in man. Magic, on the contrary, has its existence only in man. It comes forth with the breath after the performance of appropriate ritual acts.

Morals and Religion

Throughout most of Melanesia the moral and the religious systems are interrelated. The Manus of the Admiralty Islands provide the extreme case. These folk look upon the accepted code as divinely ordained, and they hold that any breach, no matter how trivial, will bring down ghostly wrath and cause the offender, or a member of his household, to fall ill.[7] Elsewhere, only some of the moral rules have supernatural validation. In Malaita it is believed that if a man were to kill a relative he would be in danger of death at the hands of the ancestors common to himself and the victim; and that if a woman were to conceal

---

[6] See, for example, R. R. Marett, 1909, and H. Hubert and M. Mauss, 1904.

an adulterous intrigue she would at her next confinement face the threat of her husband's ancestors deliberately prolonging the labor to force a confession.[8] Similarly, in Busama, New Guinea, one class of spirits is supposed to punish trespassing and another class marriage within the forbidden degrees of kinship.[9] Yet in Malaita, the ancestors ignore trespassing, and in Busama the spirits are indifferent to adultery; moreover, both communities lack extrahuman penalties for theft.

Guadalcanal is different. Here morality and religion are poles apart. The people have pronounced ideas on what constitutes wrongdoing and roundly condemn such actions as stealing, adultery, incest, and disloyalty to relatives; but they leave chastisement to the persons who have been injured and, according to the circumstances, allow them to resort to violence or to sorcery. The demands from the other world are purely ceremonial, and the villager who fulfills the normal ritual requirements is assured of support from the spirits of his clan and subclan.

It may therefore be said that Guadalcanal religion defines the relation between the natives and the world around them, confirms their hope of support from powers outside themselves, and provides a, to them, practical—even rational—method of handling the problems of disease and death. What it does not do is reinforce their notions about good and evil. Their opinions on such questions are already so strong that any additional arguments would be redundant.

Christianity

The Anglican Mission opened a church and school in Longgu around the year 1912. A serious epidemic of dysentery had occurred, and the diviners assigned anger on the part of the great spirit Luvu as the reason for it. They said that a dog had carried a turtle bone into Luvu's shrine, and the sickness was in punishment for the people's failure to expiate the sacrilege with offerings. The villagers were aggrieved at such a visitation for an act that was beyond their control, even if they had been aware that it was being committed. Two of the senior men, Tilani and Nggimo, both of whom were still alive in 1933, went over to Florida, where the headquarters of the Mission were situated, to request a native missionary. There was some delay before a suitably-trained catechist could be found, and when at last he arrived, the epidemic had subsided. Accordingly, Tilani and Nggimo, although they helped the man to build a house, did not bother to listen to his teaching. After a few months the leader of their subclan ordered him out of the hamlet. Another of the seniors then intervened with an invitation to settle near him. This man also organized the erection of a large structure to serve as a school for the children on weekdays and as a church for converts on Sundays. Soon the Mission issued a translation of the *Book of*

---

[7] R. F. Fortune, 1935.
[8] H. I. Hogbin, 1939, Chap. 4.
[9] H. I. Hogbin, 1951, Chap. 11.

Common Prayer in the Kaoka language (*Gira Na Mlai Bosa,* Norfolk Island, 1916). I did not discover who was responsible for the work, but his knowledge of the local speech was so defective that the natives found the volume incomprehensible and refused to look at it. Today the catchists, who are all from Florida, use their own Florida dialect, which is closely related to Kaoka, for church work, including teaching.

The fact that the request to the Mission came during an epidemic gives the key to why a number of the villagers have embraced Christianity. These are the folk who had the misfortune to contract a complaint that responded neither to magic nor to sacrifice. They felt that as the traditional remedies had proved unavailing, it might be to their advantage to see what the new religion could do. Other explanations for joining the congregation are the prestige of a faith supported by Europeans (whose store of possessions is accepted as irrefutable evidence of superior knowledge), the promise of eternal life, and the expectation —not yet discovered to be an illusion—of easier taboos and smaller economic cost. Then there are also a few who see a cross worn around the neck of a believer as an effective protection against *vele* sorcerers. Recently education has become more significant. The natives increasingly place a mystical valuation on the ability to read and write, and, since the Government has no funds to provide schools, the only means whereby parents can ensure learning for a child is to accept Christianity and send him to the Mission establishment.

Elsewhere in Melanesia the European missionaries' disapproval of polygamy and divorce has created opposition. Around Longgu, however, very few householders, apart from the headmen, had more than one wife, and, as we have seen, marriage has always been stable. The only persons who chafe at the regulations are those whose spouse turns out to be sterile.

Nowadays pagans and Christians alike regard both religious systems as valid. A common saying has it that if a man clings to the spirits and is prepared to make sacrifices to them, he can depend on their exercising ghostly *nanama* in his interest; but if instead he turns to the Christian God and attends church regularly, he can equally expect to receive the benefit of divine *nanama.* The two forms of otherwordly power are conceived as working in the same manner and achieving identical results.

The attitude to prayer is also a carry-over from the past. The Christians refer to their petitions as *aru,* the term for magical spell, and a man who wants something badly, whether it be the recovery of a loved one from illness or fine weather after days of tempest, begs the native catechist for God's help. Matins and evensong may be interrupted for ten minutes or more to allow for the badgering of the Almighty.

The most remarkable of the efforts at fashioning the missionaries' teachings into the familiar mold is the rejection of supernatural sanctions for the ethical rules given in the scriptures. Native Christians approve most of the Commandments and also such passages as the Sermon on the Mount; but they ignore—or perhaps fail to hear—any reference to hell-fire as punishment. They compromise on one point only: they allow for a nonhuman penalty for extramarital intercourse. A person guilty of fornication or adultery who goes to take Communion without first admitting guilt is assumed to be in danger of choking to death as he attempts to swallow the wine. Private confession always precedes the administration of the Sacrament, and worshipers and catechists said repeatedly that sexual irregularity is the only sin for which absolution is sought. Yet they could not tell me the name of anyone who had collapsed at the altar, and when a believer dies, Christians and pagans alike still give sorcery as the reason.

Religion of the Hill People

At this stage we can return with profit to the natives of the interior. Comparison reveals that their beliefs have a strong resemblance to those of the coast, but the differences of social structure already discussed have led to variation in the details of the accompanying practices.

In the hills, the same distinction is made between the greater and the lesser beings. This time it will be convenient to consider the latter first, and I shall begin with an account of the mortuary ritual.

When a person is ill and small hopes are held for his recovery, the relatives assemble to say farewell. As soon as death takes place all wail and lament until the women decide that it is time to prepare the body for public display. The widow and some of the others bathe it, shave the head, clothe it in new garments, and carry it to a pile of mats in the center of the house. The men now reenter, those most closely related bringing strings of discs, which they lay over the chest. Eventually each removes his contribution, though later the sisters' sons throw theirs into the grave or onto the funeral pyre.

News of the death is now sent out to the more distant kinsfolk, including the members of the widow's clan. The latter, on arrival at the homestead, are obliged to chide her angrily—sometimes they threaten to kill her—for not looking after her husband properly. The dead man's brothers intervene before she can come to harm and indicate that they do not hold her responsible.

The body is kept for two days and nights, and at intervals the relatives sing dirges, a set for each type of relationship: one for fathers (real and classificatory), one for mothers, one for sons, one for daughters, and so on. These are punctuated by speeches from the leaders about the virtues of the dead man and how his loss must be avenged.

Disposal is either by burial or cremation, depending on the traditions of the clan and the wishes of the deceased. For burial the body is wrapped up and carried into the bush to a spot where four men, two from each moiety, have dug the grave. They use sticks of *mbou* wood, a hard tough timber that would be ideal in house construction if it were not reserved for this digging job. The face may be turned toward the rising sun or toward the abode of the souls on the peak of Mount Nasuha.

The members of the funeral party take a ritual bath on their way home and smear their foreheads with lime. The widow retreats to the house and does not emerge for 100 days. The immediate kinsmen of the dead man now prepare a feast for the visitors. They kill most of his pigs and strip his gardens for the purpose. The sisters' sons present the gravediggers with strings of discs, and the other clansmen offer a few dog's or porpoise teeth to those who have sung the dirges.

The dead man's sisters look after the widow during her retirement, counting the days by tying knots in a piece of string. For a week she remains silent, but after that is allowed to whisper if spoken to. She also refrains from bathing, and her sisters-in-law prepare her meals from vegetables that grow wild. For this same period the other close relatives do not bathe, but they do eat ordinary food.

A month or so after the funeral the widow's brothers visit the homestead and hand the dead man's brothers several strings of discs, for which a counter-gift is immediately presented. People say that the offerings from the one side indicate sorrow and those from the other gratitude for it. Doubtless, too, they symbolize the intention of each of the parties to maintain the ties created by the union.

Sometime later the dead man's clansmen prepare a feast for the widow and repay her for the mourning with strings of discs. Most of the food she sends to her own clansmen. She is now free to rejoin her parents or, if she cares to do so, to marry again. Her kinsfolk do not expect extra gifts if a man from the first husband's clan persuades her to stay with him (though he may prefer to send them something), but a stranger is obliged to offer a few strings, both to them and to the relatives of his predecessor.

After a year the skull is disinterred. Two of the dead man's relatives go to the grave, taking along water to cleanse the bones. The digging is again done with sticks of *mbou* wood. The skull stays in the homestead for a short time and is then placed in the clan repository (called a *pe'o,* as on the coast).

If cremation is chosen instead of burial, the pyre is built in the bush and lit with a newly-kindled flame. The mourning rites and taboos follow in succession, and finally the ashes are placed in the repository.

The spirits of the dead (*tarunga*) are believed to be able to exercise supernatural power (*mana*) for the benefit of the living, and their descendants in the female line thus offer them sacrifices of pigs to secure their good will and thereby achieve material prosperity—bountiful harvests, fat pigs, success in hunting and river fishing, and good health. The ghosts of headmen are stronger than those of other people; in particular, they can use their influence to bring victory in battle. They thus become the equivalent of the warrior spirits of the coast. Each clan worships its own previous leader and presents pork prior to raiding, when threatened with enemy attack, and after returning triumphant from battle. The rites connected with the spirits of ordinary individuals also follow the familiar pattern. These are honored by their immediate clan descendants and give more personal rewards. Generally, householders delay honoring their spirits until forced into taking action by their own illness or that of a member of their family. A spirit medium is then consulted to identify the being responsible. That night he (or sometimes she) retires behind a screen in the corner of the house and, after the light has been extinguished, recites a magical formula to summon his control. He asks this spirit a number of conventional questions. Replies are given by whistles that, through some trick of ventriloquism, appear to come from the roof. A long low note indicates "yes," a short shrill blast "no." As soon as the patient or his guardian is aware of the ancestor's name, a pig is dedicated for future sacrifice.

I must emphasize that the people believe that the spirits cause illness only, never death. If someone does succumb, a sorcerer is believed to have been at work.

Naturally the shark spirits are lacking: the hill dwellers have no direct access to the sea and hence undertake neither salt-water fishing nor overseas voyaging. But every clan has its snake spirit, a female being known as a *vihona,* with an accompanying myth. A characteristic example is that relating of the arrival, sometime in the remote past, of the *vihona* Kihuimasanga together with her baby, in one of the districts. The child cried for something to eat, and she gave it vegetables from the basket she was carrying. Shortly afterwards, when it wanted to defecate, she asked some of the women to direct her to the proper place. This inquiry they could not understand: they had no food of their own and thus never ate and never had to relieve themselves. Kihuimasanga made a hole in the ground for the child's feces, which changed into yams and taro. Her basket and a stone that it contained are now preserved in a shrine, and here the headman of the clan makes offerings to secure the operation of her *mana* to cause his followers' gardens to flourish.

Men after sacrificing and women after childbirth are alike taboo and set apart, but unfortunately I failed to inquire whether they have to avoid food cooked by anyone but themselves or only that prepared by members of the opposite sex. I also cannot say for certain if menstruation renders a woman spiritually unclean, but such evidence as I have suggests that it does not.

8

Recent Changes

A T THE BEGINNING of this book I said that most of my field work in Guadalcanal was carried out thirty years ago. I mentioned, too, that my use
of the present tense when describing conditions as they were then was
purely a matter of convenience. Although I went back during World War II,
I have not returned since 1945. Not much general material has been published
on subsequent developments, and nothing at all specifically about Longgu, but
I shall now try to bring some parts of the picture up to date. It should be
pointed out immediately, however, that the Guadalcanal fighting of 1942–1943,
among the bloodiest in the Pacific campaigns, was confined to the central and
western parts of the north coast, and the people whose society I have dealt with
here did not suffer directly. None of them was shot, and their villages were
never bombed. The main hardship they experienced was the loss of manpower
after the establishment of the American base, when the adult males were con-
scripted for the labor corps.

By 1945 the traditional headmen had already disappeared. No longer
was there any occasion for the great feasts that had enabled men with ambition
to rise to the top. The efforts of the missionaries had led to the abandonment of
the pagan festivals and also to the stamping out of polygamy, which provided
the prospective leader with extra workers; and Government intervention to stop
native raiding had meant the end of the offerings to the warrior spirits and of
the great overseas trading expeditions. If items from other districts were now
required—and not many were—a single canoe set out alone without an accompanying fleet as protection. Further, even at that period no member of the older
generation was in the position to demand obedience from his juniors. The
elders lost their monopoly of the wealth as soon as the youths began earning
wages from employment on the plantations, and once a person had become a
Christian, he accepted individual responsibility for his actions and ceased to
depend on sacrifices carried out by other people. Finally, the Langalanga Lagoon
natives had given up the manufacture of shell discs.[1]

---

[1] C. S. Belshaw, 1950, pp. 179, 180.

At first the Administration experimented by appointing an ex-police officer as its representative in each series of villages. Some of these men tried to do their job conscientiously, but too often they relied upon official backing and degenerated into petty despots.

At length, towards the end of the war, a determined step was taken to return to the past and give the natives a greater say in the running of their affairs. Recognition was given to the principal men of the smaller social units such as the hamlets or subclans, and in each administrative subdistrict patrol officers encouraged them to set up a council and a court. Today the councils consist of those elders recommended for appointment by the Government representative. He presides over the meetings, which he calls regularly at intervals of about a month, when matters of common policy are discussed and principles established for transmission to the European district commissioner.

The Government representative also sits as president of the court, a body consisting of himself, a clerk, and six elders nominated by the council. It deals with criminal, civil, and native customary cases. Serious crimes (such as murder, rape, and incest) must be brought before a magistrate or judge, but the villagers have jurisdiction in matters where adequate punishment does not exceed a fine of 14 dollars (5 pounds sterling) or imprisonment for one month. Similarly, in civil disputes the property in question must have a maximum value of 28 dollars (10 pounds sterling). From decisions in customary cases there is no appeal, but persons found guilty of a crime or a civil offense, if dissatisfied with the verdict, can appeal to the district commissioner for a new trial.

Convicts are either sent to the Government station to serve their sentences or kept in the subdistrict. If the term is for a few days only, they are allowed to sleep at home but from dawn to dark have to carry out work like road-making that will be of benefit to everybody.[2]

Progress in other spheres has been less rapid. The difficulty is that before the Solomon Islands can become economically viable—and without this, full political freedom, without strings attached, is in the modern world meaningless—tremendous expenditure is required to pay for the education of the population, the maintenance of a full-scale public health service, the inauguration of a system of transportation, and the setting up of research organizations to investigate the manifold problems of agriculture and marketing. To date, the metropolitan power has made little money available. The result is that only a handful of men have had training, and the coconut remains the principal commercial crop. The bulk of the islanders continue to live as subsistence horticulturalists. They grow the old foods according to the same methods as their ancestors, tend pigs and go fishing, and dwell in houses built in the traditional style. Cooperation is as essential now as it was a century ago, and kinship still provides the essential framework for all the working groups.

The natives have reacted to the state of stagnation by embracing a millen-

---

[2] Councils and courts were set up in the Longgu area in 1945, but I have heard no reports of how they are succeeding. Those of northern Malaita are discussed in H. I. Hogbin, 1944, pp. 257 to 283, and 1945, pp. 61 to 69.

ary cult that they call Masinga Rule, a name that many of the European settlers imagine to be derived from "Marxian" or perhaps "Marching," though in fact it means "brotherhood" in one of the dialects. The believers hold that, if they behave themselves in the manner divinely revealed to the leaders, the wartime American transports will return bringing all the goods of Western manufacture that are so ardently desired. The movement has affinities with manifestations in other parts of Melanesia, notably New Guinea, except that there the ancestors are revered as the source of the wealth that is to come.[3]

In the beginning, native objectives were entirely political. They wanted an administrative and judicial system that was completely their own. The Malaita folk, for example, divided their island into nine districts, each under a "head chief." Six of these men were mission teachers, and all were powerful. They ran their affairs independently, but from time to time met and discussed matters of common interest. The hierarchy under them consisted of "full chiefs," "leader chiefs," and "line chiefs," all of them assisted by clerks who were responsible for the dispatch of instructions, listing the members, and codifying the rules that were to be obeyed (these were for the most part Puritanical in inspiration). A bodyguard of youths armed with truncheons supported the most senior chiefs. These "duties," as they were called, when not engaged in Masinga-Rule tasks, were drilled by "strife chiefs," who functioned as corporals and sergeants.

The next step was an order to build "towns." Groups that were living in the forests uprooted themselves and descended to the beach, where they laid out settlements with streets crossing at right angles in the manner of an army camp. The residents cultivated collective gardens under the direction of "farmer chiefs," who divided the produce among the individual households. They also built great meeting houses where high officials of the Masinga Rule could entertain, debate their aims, and hear cases.

The more mystical aspects of the cult then came to be stressed. The generous American soldiers were distinguished from the niggardly British plantation owners of the pre- and postwar years, and the dogma was propounded that, if only the people had sufficient faith and carried out the ritual outlined by the Masinga-Rule chiefs, the former would come back to the Solomons with their landing craft and liberty ships. These would anchor in the harbors and unload cases full of cigarettes, tobacco, canned foods, axes, knives, machines, fishhooks, lines, clothing, and all the other things that had been there for the asking from 1943 to 1945. Fired with enthusiasm, the natives erected huge sheds for storing the cargo. Sceptics, they said, would be deprived of their land and punished.

The origin of this and similar movements is to be sought in the incompatibility of wants and the means of achieving them. The islanders can take no practical steps to bridge the gap. They lack the resources and opportunity for making the goods or for obtaining them from outside. In the past, crises of

---

[3] See P. Worsley, 1957; L. P. Mair, 1957, pp. 175 to 182, and 1959, pp. 113 to 136; H. I. Hogbin, 1958, Chap. 8; T. Schwartz, 1962; and P. Lawrence, *Road Belong Cargo,* Manchester University Press, forthcoming.

this kind were resolved by an appeal to religion. When common sense and experience had been utilized to the full and the outcome of an enterprise was still in doubt, the people enlisted aid from the world of the supernatural by means of a sacrifice. The present appeal to faith and ritual has therefore ample precedent.

What is surprising is the degree of organization, which ten or even five years previously nobody would have thought possible. The inhabitants of wide areas have come together, using pidgin English as a means of communication, and have subordinated their traditional enmities to the common cause. The movement may be regarded as the forerunner of Solomon-Island nationalism.

In the earlier stages the followers of Masinga Rule quietly declined to carry out Government orders or to enter employment on the reopened plantations. But after a time, the leaders felt strong enough to make demands. They called together a series of gatherings, which thousands attended, and made threats against not only the men who would not join them but also against the Europeans. The Administration tried to be conciliatory and enlist native cooperation, but was eventually forced to make mass arrests. What the upshot will be it as yet too soon to say.

References Cited and Recommended Reading

BELSHAW, C. S., 1950, "Changes in Heirloom Jewellery in the Solomon Islands," *Oceania,* Vol. 20.

———, 1954, *Changing Melanesia.* New York: Oxford University Press.
The economics of social change in Melanesia.

BERNATZIK, H. A., 1936, *Owa Raha.* Vienna: Bernina Verlag.
An account of the natives of Santa Anna, southern Solomons.

BOGESI, G., 1948, "Santa Isabel," *Oceania,* Vol. 18.
The society of the natives of Ysabel, written by one of them.

BLACKWOOD, B., 1935, *Both Sides of Buka Passage.* New York: Oxford University Press.
The natives of the small islands between Buka and Bougainville, northern Solomons.

CODERE, H., 1950, "Fighting with Property," *Monograph of the American Ethnological Society,* Vol. 18.

CODRINGTON, R. H., 1891, *The Melanesians.* New York: Oxford University Press. (Reprinted by Behavior Science Reprints, New Haven: Human Relations Area Files Press, 1957.)
The only general account of the native cultures of the Solomons, Banks, and New Hebrides. One of the classics of anthropology.

FIRTH, R., 1940, "The Analysis of Mana," *Journal of the Polynesian Society,* Vol. 49.

FOX, C. E., 1924, *Threshold of the Pacific.* London: Routledge.
An account of the peoples of San Cristoval.

———, 1962, *Kakamora.* London: Hodder.

EVANS-PRITCHARD, E. E., 1940, *The Nuer.* New York: Oxford University Press.

FORTUNE, R. F., 1932, *Sorcerers of Dobu.* London: Routledge.
A study of a matrilineal community from an island off the east coast of New Guinea.

———, 1935, *Manus Religion.* Philadelphia: American Philosophical Society, Memoir No. 3.

HOCART, A. M., 1922, "Cult of the Dead in Eddystone Island," *Journal of the Royal Anthropological Institute,* Vol. 52.
The religious system of a people in the central Solomons.

HOGBIN, H. I., 1936a, "Sorcery and Administration," *Oceania*, Vol. 6.
Includes several photographs taken in Longgu and Nangali.
———, 1936b, "Mana," *Oceania*, Vol. 6.
A comparative study of the religions of four island communities. Includes photographs taken in Longgu and Nangali.
———, 1938, "Social Advancement in Guadalcanal," *Oceania*, Vol. 8.
Includes ten photographs taken in Longgu.
———, 1939, *Experiments in Civilization*. London: Routledge.
The culture of the To'ambaita people of Malaita, with a consideration of the effects of European contact.
———, 1944, "Native Councils and Native Courts in the Solomon Islands," *Oceania*, Vol. 14.
———, 1945, "Notes and Instructions to Native Administrations in the Solomon Islands," *Oceania*, Vol. 16.
———, 1951, *Transformation Scene*. London: Routledge.
The effects of European contact on the culture of the people of Busama village, northeastern New Guinea.
———, 1958, *Social Change*. London: Watts.
Three chapters are devoted to the changes brought about by European contact among the Melanesians generally. Seven of the photographs were taken in or near Longgu.
———, 1963, *Kinship and Marriage in a New Guinea Village*. London: Athlone Press.
The stable elements in the culture of Busama (see Hogbin, H. I., 1951).
HUBERT, H., and M. MAUSS, 1904, "La Magie," *L'Année Sociologique*. Paris: Alcan.
IVENS, W. G., 1927, *Melanesians of the South-Eastern Solomons*. London: Routledge.
The cultures of the natives of Sa'a and Ulawa, Malaita.
———, 1930, *Island Builders of the Pacific*. London: Seeley Service.
The culture of the natives of the lagoon islets off the northeastern coast of Malaita.
———, 1934, "A Grammar of the Language of Longgu," *Bulletin of the School of Oriental Studies*, Vol. 7.
———, 1937, "A Vocabulary of the Language of Longgu," *Bulletin of the School of Oriental Studies*, Vol. 9.
LEACH, E. R., 1958, "Concerning Trobriand Clans and the Kinship Category of *Tabu*," in J. Goody (ed.), *The Development Cycle in Domestic Groups*. Cambridge, England: University Press.
———, 1961, *Rethinking Anthropology*. London: Athone Press.
MAIR, L. P., 1958, "The Pursuit of the Millennium in Melanesia," *British Journal of Sociology*, Vol. 9.
———, 1959, "Independent Religious Movements in Three Continents," *Comparative Studies in Society and History*, Vol. 1.
MALINOWSKI, B., 1922, *Argonauts of the Western Pacific*. New York: Dutton.

Trading voyages and ceremonial currency among the matrilineal Trobriand Islanders.

———, 1926, *Crime and Custom in Savage Society*. London: Routledge.
The jural system of the Trobriand Islanders.

———, 1929, *Sexual Life of Savages in North-Western Melanesia*. London: Routledge.
Courtship and marriage among the Trobrianders.

———, 1935, *Coral Gardens and their Magic*. London: G. Allen.
Agriculture, economics, and religion among the Trobrianders.

———, 1948, *Magic, Science, and Religion*. New York: Free Press.
Several essays on the Trobrianders, mainly about religion.

MARETT, R. R., 1909, *Threshold of Religion*. London: Methuen.

OLIVER, D. L., 1955, *A Solomon Island Society*. Cambridge, Mass: Harvard University Press.
A detailed account of the Siuai people of Bougainville, northwestern Solomons. They are matrilineal but have a different structure from that found in Longgu.

RIVERS, W. H. R., 1914, *History of Melanesian Society*. Cambridge, England: University Press.
The first volume gives notes on various Melanesian peoples, including some of the neighbors of the Longgu villagers. The information was collected from individual mission teachers, who were interviewed aboard ship as Rivers traveled through the islands. The second volume is concerned with the conjectural migrations into the area. It may be read either as a warning of how not to study anthropology or as a more or less entertaining fairy tale.

ROBINSON, M. S., 1962, "Complimentary Filiation and Marriage in the Trobriands," in M. Fortes (ed.), *Marriage in Tribal Societies*. Cambridge, England: University Press.

SCHWARTZ, T., "The Paliau Movement in the Admiralty Islands, 1946–54," *Anthropological Papers of the American Museum of Natural History*, Vol. 49, Pt. 2.

UBEROI, J. P. SINGH, 1962, *Politics of the Kula Ring*. Manchester, England: University Press.
More about the Trobrianders, based on a re-examination of Malinowski's published work.

WORSLEY, P., 1957, *The Trumpet Shall Sound*. London: Macgibbon and Kee.

Glossary
of Anthropological Terms

These definitions are based on those given in *Notes and Queries in Anthropology,* Sixth Edition, 1951, published by Routledge & Kegan Paul Ltd., London, for the Royal Anthropological Institute. They follow the established usages of British anthropologists.

AFFINES: Relatives by marriage. Affines are of two types, the cognates of the person's spouse (for example, his wife's brother) and the spouses of his own cognates (for example, his brother's wife).

CLAN: A group of persons of both sexes with obligations of an exclusive kind: membership of the group is determined by unilineal descent, actual or putative. Clans may be either localized (as when all, or a great many, adult members of one sex live together in an area recognized as clan territory) or dispersed (as when the members of both sexes are scattered through an extensive district).

COGNATES: Persons descended from the same ancestor. (Cognates who trace descent from the same ancestor through males exclusively are known as *agnates,* a term not required in this book.)

CROSS-COUSINS: A person's father's sisters' children and mother's brothers' children.

DESCENT: The recognized connection between a person and his ancestors.

EXOGAMY: The rule prohibiting marriage within a specified group (for example, the clan).

MATRILATERAL: On the mother's side. MATRILATERAL KIN: The cognates on the mother's side.

MATRILINEAL: Traced through females only. MATRILINEAL KIN: The cognates to whom a person is related exclusively through females. (N.B. The matrilineal kinsfolk constitute a small section of the matrilateral kinsfolk.)

PARALLEL COUSINS: A person's father's brothers' children and mother's sisters' children.

PATRILATERAL: On the father's side. PATRILATERAL KIN: The cognates on the father's side.

PATRILINEAL: Traced through males only. PATRILINEAL KIN: The cognates to whom a person is related exclusively through males. (N.B. The patrilineal kinsfolk constitute a small section of the patrilateral kinsfolk.)

TOTEM: The natural species, natural phenomenon, or object with which the members of the group (for example, the clan) have a ritual relation.

UNILINEAL: Traced through a line of males exclusively or through a line of females exclusively. UNILINEAL GROUP: A group of which membership is determined by unlineal descent (for example, the clan).

UTERINE KIN: The cognates to whom a person is related through females.